Farming For Ever

Patrick Evans

Published by
Sapey Press
Whitbourne
Worcester
WR6 5ST

Telephone 01886 821674

© Patrick Evans 1996

ISBN 0-9528916-0-3

A full CIP record for this book is available
from the British Library

Cover illustration by Bill Cameron-Johnson

Text design and typesetting in Garamond by Dexter Haven, London

Printing by Ipswich Book Company, Ipswich

H 113,290 |630
£5.00

To Kristin

*who successfully combines
the dual role of unfailing
supporter and invaluable critic*

Contents

Author's Preface

I would like to express my thanks to Kristin, my wife who has seen the manuscript through each fresh stage in the long period of gestation. Also her nephew, Robert Hastings, who has masterminded the production of the book, and Bill Cameron-Johnson, for his excellent cover design.

In the development of the text, I must take full responsibility for the final result, but would like to express my debt to many friends for their help with a critical assessment both of the subject matter and my use of the English language. Among those who have read the manuscript in full or particular chapters, I would like to thank most warmly Edward Goulding, Professor Sir Colin Spedding, Geoffrey Wilkinson, Michael Smith, Hugh Nowell, Elizabeth Locke, Dr Robin Mowat, Alec Hutton, Dr Ian Robertson, Dr Jameson Bell, Adrian Friggens, Malcolm Rankin and my brother, Robin Evans. The road from conception to completion has demanded more stamina than I had expected, and all have helped in moving things forward.

As I have endeavoured to make clear, this book is not an attempt at an exhaustive study of the present situation in agriculture. It is more an exploration of some of the longer-term perspectives, and how they seem to link together through some of the events I have experienced in my farming life. There is undoubtedly a need today to examine the foundations of farming, and consider the contribution they can make to a world in need of a satisfying way of life for every nation. So this is a contribution to a dialogue which is already under way.

Patrick Evans
Haytons
Whitbourne

Foreword
Lord Plumb, DL, MEP, FRAgS

Pat Evans makes a unique contribution to a better understanding of human endeavour to care for the countryside, and he expresses so clearly, over a world canvas, the important role farming families can play in today's society.

He makes it clear, however, that farming is not just a way of life, with spiritual foundations and moral values, but also a business under pressure from current economic theories.

One farmer's perception of the forces at work in this century, and the consideration which would seem to count most in the next, is a vision which can only be written from experience through travel and contacts, and it reflects a common purpose for mankind.

So *Farming For Ever*, Pat explains, aims to be an examination of the possibilities and some of the grounds for hope. To reaffirm the long-term future may in itself carry a challenge for the contemporary scene.

He reminds us that it was in times of adversity that friendships grew up between technician and farmer, which should be a lesson for many of the poorer countries around the world, 'hands on' approach as distinct from bureaucracy.

It was from the initiative of one of my illustrious predecessors in the NFU, Lord Netherthorpe, that the International Federation of Agricultural Producers was created, and Pat refers to the creation of this worldwide organisation of farm leaders which, 50 years on from its foundation, now covers the interests of 86 countries. Many of the hopes and ambitions of the Founding Fathers have not materialised, since half the world's population is still hungry, but this does not detract from the aims or the achievements of such a worldwide representative body of the families of the land.

The author reminds us that IFAP remains largely unrecognised and unsung by grass-roots farmers in most countries. Had it been able to articulate a more united purpose, there is no doubt it would have had a greater impact.

In farming, people have always mattered, and it is interesting to be reminded of the Tolpuddle Martyrs, the first farm workers' union, founded by Joseph Arch in 1872.

The dialogue at international level, between farm and farm workers' leaders, is important, but there is no industry where the relationship between employer and employee is more important.

Peter Howard obviously had a considerable influence on Pat, and made a decisive impact on his thinking and living. He would be proud of this book, relating much of the work of one of his students. He covers his canvas with such interesting anecdotes and wisdom of many issues facing all of us.

He reminds us that when it comes to human nature, the real expert is God!

Today, with biotechnology beckoning, and talk of genetic engineering, mixing expectation with trepidation, we have to learn to view the future from a new angle.

It would be folly to see agricultural research mark time, or even diminish, at a moment when considerable expansion is so badly needed.

I thoroughly recommend this book to every student of the history of agriculture and rural life, and those who care for future development, and congratulate my good friend and colleague, Pat Evans, for such a fine contribution.

Chapter 1
Farming Perspectives –
a World Canvas

Historically, farming fortunes have been looked at in Britain mainly from the European angle, and certainly the Western angle. As farmers, we have become conversant with the problems of farming in temperate climates, but have till recently largely neglected the tropics. Looking at the overall industrial development of the last century, we have been content to see people getting sucked into the cities because there has been work for them to do. While back in the countryside, mechanisation has led to a steady rise both in productivity and overall production, as science has made an increasing contribution.

As the inhuman working conditions and slums were grappled with, full employment was on everyone's lips as the great social achievement so near our grasp. The eclipse of heavy industry by the new age of the microchip and the decay of the inner cities have undermined the old certainties, and shattered confidence in our ultimate goals. The economic strength of Japan is held up as an example, mainly on the grounds of its evident success, though we have indeed also learned useful lessons from the Japanese on the breaking down of class barriers, the development of consensus and the practice of a total quality approach. But while the Japanese have pushed the possibilities of economic development to its limits, they may be about to demonstrate that the limits to competition globally are going to be reached before the limits to growth.

Meanwhile, farmers have become increasingly aware of their dwindling numbers, an awareness brought home at first by a decline in their influence on the political scene, and latterly by the realisation that the rural population is under threat. Some villages have grown, including my own of Whitbourne, to the great benefit of community life. But at the same time one is acutely aware that agriculture, even in the village, remains very much a minority interest. The variety of food on offer may be making an impression, at least if one is to judge by a growing interest in the classier restaurants and the plethora of cookery books. But the essential link with the land has been cut, and is only being remade by the opening of a number of farms to the public and to school visits, and by a growing concern for access to the countryside.

In these circumstances, the discovery of tropical and semitropical agriculture is a new world for the average British farmer. I omit for the moment the utterly horrific scenes of poverty and famine frequently brought to our television screens. In any case, as often as not, they reflect the ravages of civil war even more than climatic difficulties, and it is quite breathtaking for the ordinary farmer to glimpse the full potential of the sun's power in stimulating growth around the year. Not only can several crops be grown in the space of one calendar year, but the speed of growth which this implies is a revelation to those accustomed to sow in October and reap the following August. Then it dawns that the great essential to realise this potential is water. Good water management is the key to production, and in some cases even to survival, while the rate at which organic matter in the soil is oxidised means that frequently such soils become destabilised and subject to serious erosion. In brief, it is exciting, and therefore a particular challenge to those accustomed to a slower natural rhythm.

The other striking feature is the number of people involved in farming and the smallness of their farms. Farmers in China and India are numbered not just in their millions, but in their hundreds of millions. Irene Laure, a pioneer of reconciliation between the French and German peoples after the war, said of India, that if you haven't been there, you haven't seen humanity. Suddenly one sees farming as still the majority occupation for the inhabitants of our planet: perhaps a part of the spearhead rather than the rearguard, as sometimes assumed. Certainly it must be a major factor in any new social development, with land so intensively occupied that there is scarcely room for large-scale concepts, though plenty of place for what has been wisely dubbed appropriate technology. The first thing to understand is that these farmers are an asset and not a problem, a perception so often clouded by the sponsors of birth control programmes, however necessary those may be. These farmers are not waiting to be planned into a new pattern, but joined in the search for the right way ahead.

A generation back, the received wisdom was that industrialisation held the key to development and modernisation. Many newly independent countries went for prestige industrial projects, and were fully backed by Western opinion and investment. The wheel has come full circle and perceptions have changed but there is probably still an unjustified assumption that the Western World is in the vanguard of progress simply because of its technological achievements. The nature of spiritual values may be beginning to attract fresh exploration, and this will hopefully be hastened by those who have lived under communist régimes. But it is a long step further to focus on this direction for our future, and in particular for our next steps in the present.

Malcolm Muggeridge once wrote, 'It has always seemed to me that the most interesting thing in the world is to try and understand what life is about…' It was in that spirit that I entered farming, and I can remember my disappointment, on switching to studying science at school, to find that science could answer the question how but not the question why. We are left to grapple with that question in all human activities and all our different societies. Perhaps today there are simply too few who do stop to ask why. This is not the moment for philosophising, but it is worth remembering how easily we fall into habits of thought and the acceptance of existing patterns. The newly industrialised countries of Asia are hailed because they are part of a pattern we can understand. We salute their progress on the road to wealth, and we almost instinctively feel that they represent the pattern for further development. Yet I couldn't help but be struck by the words of Allan Griffith, Australian diplomat and political adviser to several Prime Ministers, when speaking at a meeting of Pacific nations in Vancouver of, 'those nations in need who want to see a world economy which works for them, and not just a world economy based on throwing motor cars at each other in some mad fetish to compete'.

In the same vein it sometimes seems that Green campaigners spend more time wrestling with different aspects of Creation than pondering the purposes of the Creator. It is easy to understand the need and the struggle to get these items onto the political agenda as a high priority. But are Green politics necessarily the best way to achieve this? There is a certain assumption that if you have a cause, the obvious course is to set up an organisation to promote and pursue it. The assumption has a degree of logic and the cause can be quickly publicised that way. Yet there are drawbacks when such organisations proliferate and there is no central purpose to hold them together. Established political parties are accepted as having a central purpose and a full range of policies. So the alternative way is to win them to take on board the urgency of environmental considerations. Many Greens seem to feel this to be in large degree a waste of breath. They see themselves almost as a race apart, apostles of their cause in a materialist and uncaring society. But whatever the truth of this, they have to face the old saying, 'You can plan a new world on paper, but you have to build it out of people'. Can the threat of a hole in the ozone layer move people to basic change in the way they live, even if the threat implies the end of the world? The men with sandwich boards could probably tell you that it won't, but they may still feel its worth trying to make the connection. Yet it is folly to suppose that it is possible to define an acceptable life-style and then push people into conforming with it. They must be brought to an understanding of the choices involved, because only then can their wills be engaged.

The underlying truth is that, while we may be stewards of our planet, we are not in charge of the universe. It is a timely irony that the Russian cosmonaut who returned to a post-communist hero's welcome was marooned in space for lack of the cash to fetch him home. Yet a common purpose must owe more to inspiration than the means we have at our disposal. Conviction tends to override rules and to break through the horizon of what is possible. But it is usually the fruit of reflection and of a deeper understanding of the meaning of our destiny.

Anyone who lives in the countryside must be moved to reflect on the power of silence, and I think here of some of those who come to the pool on our farm to fish. Many work in factories, and all value the peace and quiet which the country offers them at a weekend. One such was Bill Taylor, sheet metal worker and convenor for his union at the then Austin works in Longbridge, Birmingham. I remember him telling me how much the quiet of the pool side meant to him, and how he wouldn't be the least bit worried if he never saw a fish! Perhaps this was partly because he had other fish to fry. He had begun to seek in silence God's prompting on his life and work, and what was right for the way ahead. On one occasion in the factory when he withdrew to one side to try and sort out a problem, he sat with his head in his hands to shut out the noise, until one of his friends came over to enquire if he was ill. So I was interested to learn that, when the Birmingham pub bombing took place, it was he who coped with the reactions at the factory. Feelings were running high and outlets for demonstration and protest were sought. Even normally assertive trade unionists were at a loss about what to do. They appealed to Bill, and though no more sure about the situation than they, he was not one to shrink from grappling with the realities of human nature. The thought came to him to lead the crowd round the block in a peaceful march. Wondering how to wind things up on their return to the factory, he had the further idea to lead them in saying the Lord's Prayer. So it was with those words of prayer for direction and forgiveness that they broke up.

Despite the emphasis on business efficiency in farming today, it may not be too fanciful to see farming as a potential factor in this process of reflection. A former French Minister of Agriculture, Edgard Pisani, in discussing the kind of agriculture that we want, weighed up the tradition that we may be about to break. 'Only yesterday, nearly everywhere in the Old Continent, farming's eternal story was part of a sacred heritage. The farmer was the priest who renewed each day by his work the basic link which exists between man and nature, between men and God. It was through him that we got our daily bread. He was the intermediary on whom life depended. It is from these images slowly modified through the years that our mental furniture has grown, our culture and all that has shaped our nature. Europe should say if she wants to turn her back on this perception of the world' (*Le Monde*, November 1994).

None would deny that farming is a business shaped by the same economic laws as any other, but it is also different. Most obviously, whatever farmers plan and do, yields and results are influenced by the weather, in other words by factors outside our control. Also, a farmer is not out just to squeeze the most he can from his land today but to pass it on in good heart to his successors. All of which means that farming is about the long term, an attitude which, if some find it slow, at least ensures a link with lasting values.

These values are shared by farmers worldwide regardless of culture or circumstances. This is illustrated by an experience I had a few years ago when introduced to a farmer in Thailand. He had a prosperous business growing tamarinds and had built up a sizeable orchard. He was a real enthusiast for his product, and propagated young trees to sell to others. He must have had a substantial influence on tamarind production both locally and further afield, for he had also developed a useful export trade. At one point quite early in the conversation, my wife Kristin referred to the economic struggles we were having with farming in Europe, and the difficulties of making an adequate profit. But she added that, whatever the difficulties, we were committed to farming and found it a really satisfying way of life, even if not the most profitable. When this was translated to him, he immediately seized my hand and pumped it up and down vigorously, because the sentiments expressed chimed so exactly with his own. I felt at once that it justified my faith in the values that farmers share worldwide, and the belief that they can be a bridgehead in establishing an acceptable North/South rapprochement and a true understanding for the future.

It may seem a big assumption to make, but the truth is that we are all developing nations on the road to what, for want of a better phrase, one might call the first world civilisation. Communications are making it possible, perhaps almost inevitable, if we are to succeed in living at peace. It may be no more than common sense to think that farmers can play a part in bringing this about, if they do not entirely lose faith in their destiny. At the least it is an idea worth exploring.

Chapter 2
Current Considerations

To begin this exploration, the belief that farming has a special part to play between the rich and poor nations may be a starting point. Closing the economic gap has been high on the political agenda since the publication of the Brandt Report. The early assumptions that development depended on manufacturing industry presupposed a stable agricultural base and a climate for investment that would attract outside capital. In many cases these requirements were manifestly lacking, and the land was by far the most promising source of wealth. This is no less true because it has remained too long unrecognised.

It is not hard for western farmers to appreciate the havoc wrought on farmers elsewhere by the fluctuations in commodity markets. Primary products and raw materials have over the years lost value in real terms. International Commodity Agreements have failed to manage things better, and the markets have not delivered the improvements sometimes forecast. Western farmers and farm workers, though earning less than their industrial counterparts, have been protected from economic disaster by subsidies. So it is a bitter irony that the dumping which has resulted from the way these subsidies have been handled, should have added to the suffering of colleagues in Africa and other continents. Moreover, in Britain, where farmers have dwindled to just over 2% of the population, the food industry has flourished, with 14% of total employment, and contributing 9% to the Gross National Product. Developing countries badly need such food industries, with their potential for added value.

It is now common knowledge that despite much effort and a few successes, the gap between rich and poor nations is actually increasing. There are various reasons for this, but the fact remains that, for many, faith in the future has been undermined if not destroyed. As one who has worked for a good many years to develop and strengthen farmer to farmer links between different countries, I am convinced that a common purpose can be forged. But it is sobering to find that even some of those with whom one has worked closely believe it almost impossible that we can ever establish a converging course through current agricultural policies. It may well be that they are right, without changes of a fundamental and even revolutionary nature, and that is the field which we have to explore.

Meanwhile, environmental considerations add a further element to the pressures for a change of direction. This is emphasised by the Agenda 21 document which came out of the Rio Summit meeting in 1992, and in which agriculture takes up the most space. For some people, science and technology are among the chief villains, when they could equally well lead to a new way of doing things. Certainly the rich countries have led the way in pollution and lack of consideration for the environment, and often find it costly to restore the balance. But it does seem that in many cases redemptive policies are under way, and even the car makers are talking of technology which not only reduces fuel consumption, but actually assists in clearing the atmosphere. All of which can hopefully be of assistance to countries at an earlier stage of development. But until these things are realised in practice, it ill behoves Westerners to point the finger at those who are following in their footsteps. It has apparently not yet dawned on us that consumerism involves a constant narrowing of man's understanding on these issues, whereas pursuit of truth demands a constant and sometimes painful enlargement of that understanding. That is the real point of a longer-term perspective.

When it comes to the means needed to achieve long term ends, democracy appears to be the only possible avenue. So talk of extending democratic practice and values should not be discounted as so much window-dressing. Whatever imperfections there may be, and they will be legion, democracy in the sense of the expression of the will of the people, remains the best hope. It is the key not only to extending human rights and freedom but to developing that maturity in debate which will ultimately ensure that the truth prevails, whatever setbacks there may be in the short term. In this sense we should be clear that democracy is about much more than a parliamentary form of government, and that all forms of arriving freely at consensus are an illustration of the democratic way. Violence is quickly and rightly recognised as an affront to democracy, as are all forms of financial corruption. But it is not always so well understood that the true democrat must live what he talks about, and stand for clear moral standards and the higher authority of God or conscience over man-made laws. That respected pioneer of the European Union, Robert Schuman, wrote: 'Democracy and her freedoms can be saved only by the quality of the men who speak in her name.'

It is clear, however, that democracy evolves over time, and needs time to evolve. The frequent arguments over decentralisation in a variety of different situations should not obscure the value of the principle. It is also reinforced by the observation in the development field that the most lasting and healthy growth takes place from the bottom up, rather than from the top down. Those who have the chance to make choices in their lives should be in the business of making those choices available to others. It is a far-reaching aim but by no means simply a Utopian ideal. It involves giving a voice to those who have never had one before. It can be realised, and the growth of works councils and other forms of industrial democracy bear witness to it.

This underlines the point that democracy is not about unanimity but about healthy dialogue where minority opinions are respected even when they do not carry the day. Then, in the end, the debate should lead us to reflect more deeply on the purity of our motives. That is why a certain selflessness is needed and, in technical matters, an ability to listen to expert evidence with true objectivity. That is how sincere and determined opponents may each contribute to the ultimate triumph of the truth, as long as they never pull the shutters down on the horizon, but seek only the enlargement of understanding.

Although such understanding will clearly help in dealing with the poverty, cruelty and injustice so evident today, it is also clear that it requires a change of heart of a fundamental nature. But in assessing the contribution which farming can make, I do not want to imply that farmers are in any way better than other people. As the old farming proverb had it: 'Live as though you would die tomorrow, but farm as though you would live for ever'. In that sense farmers are the inheritors of a tradition which is not lightly derailed by the current trends of a single century, and there may be worthwhile conclusions to be drawn from it for today.

In the first place, farming is a way of life which must have spiritual foundations and moral values to function properly. It is also, of course, a business very much under pressure from current economic theories. But it is the way of life which may carry the most important message for the world today, and which farmers may need to guard most jealously. It has been suggested that there is now a desire to return to the truth by those who are tired of ideology, and a way of life can encompass that desire without being tied to the past. Those Green campaigners who call most resolutely for a new lifestyle, often seem to imagine that it can be defined and almost imposed on people by the sheer force of argument. But a way of life is an organic growth which takes time to develop and which reaches out into every phase of our existence: economic, political, cultural and environmental.

It is many-sided and constantly evolving in step with history, but its changes depend on an authority that is above Man himself. Such an authority may be variously seen as God or Conscience or even some abstract philosophical absolute, but without it there is no mainspring to living. So an examination of the farmers' way of life is fully relevant to questions about what we are living for. It is the background from which a new purpose can be born, and which is even now evident in the soul-searching being conducted in so many situations where previously accepted norms are being questioned.

In many ways, for example, the fervour being put into campaigns for animal rights can be seen as a substitute for religion in a secular age. As with religion, there can be a messianic zeal which goes completely over the top in its intolerance of other people, and which clings to some particular truth as to a personal possession. But unlike the religious, secular movements lack any divine authority which may in time bring extreme reactions back into balance, and help the zealots recognise the need for a different approach. Since moral values are essential to any valid way of life, perhaps the thought of farming as a work which goes on for ever may offer a useful corrective. Certainly it can be demonstrated that the farming way touches all aspects of life, and perhaps even poses the need for religion, if that is judged as the quest for a Creator, rather than simply as an institution.

To assess the state of farming and its future, it is then necessary to examine all these questions and how the development of science, economics and education have impinged on them. But this is not intended to be a book which makes such a comprehensive effort at a considered judgement. Rather it is one farmer's perceptions of the forces at work in this century, and the considerations which would seem to count most in the next. These perceptions will of necessity be piecemeal, and some of the opinions expressed fallible, but that need not detract from the aim of contributing towards a common purpose for mankind. In that sense we can all be servants of the truth and meditate on the purification of motive needed even to achieve some of the immediate objectives on which we are agreed. Christmas Humphreys, in his book *The Buddhist Way of Life*, says: 'Meditation is the royal highway to Man's understanding of himself'. He goes on to examine the concept of 'illumined thinking' through intuition, and postulates the thought that a man believes in a doctrine, when he behaves as if it were true. One doesn't need to be a Buddhist to recognise some truth in this!

Given this background, there is often in farming a sense of calling which has been lost in more urban environments. Despite the fact that the majority of farmers are born into farming and many are without alternative choices, farming comes to exert a particular hold. Whether this hold is seen as restrictive or liberating mainly depends on the chances of farmers finding a creative role in shaping the society of the future. Apart from a difference in its purely economic success, the Capitalist Collective may prove as stultifying as the Communist Collective in terms of human development. Our efforts to prevent the establishment of a monopoly in the marketplace reflect this anxiety. It is essential to pursue the possibility for change and, paradoxically, all the more so when changes are in fact happening quite quickly. It becomes all too easy to jump on a bandwagon without making any personal assessment of the issues, but there must always be the chance to repent at leisure!

At a time when the rising world population casts a major shadow over future developments, the key question may not be the level at which that rise is halted but rather whether poorer economies can progress peacefully without a major dislocation of society. The weight of expert opinion seems to be that the world is capable of producing food for the extra billions, but that is a very long way from seeing that it reaches those in need. With any of the scenarios on offer, it would seem that some basic change in human motivation will be necessary. It is no good appealing to enlightened self-interest when dedicated selflessness is what is needed to provide new leadership. To believe that something can happen is a beginning, but dedication and commitment are required to see it through. It is not so much a career as a task for life.

So *Farming For Ever* aims to be an examination of the possibilities, and some of the grounds for hope. Perhaps this lies not so much in terms of programmes as of people, and the human qualities which shine through the past as well as illuminating the present and the future. It may well seem that the farming tradition is an inadequate scaffolding to support such an imposing task. But a tradition that has been rooted in the centuries is not lightly washed away by successive waves of modernisation. The power of natural regeneration and rebirth can still make its mark. The prophet voices may seem to be raised against hopeless odds but if they survive historically they are not in vain, since they still have resonance for us today. To reaffirm the long-term future may in itself carry a challenge for the contemporary scene.

Chapter 3
A Personal Perspective

My early memories are marked by the belated effort of the Government in the 1930s to rescue farming from oblivion. This was mainly enshrined in the establishment of Marketing Boards, which were created to buy and market farmers' produce. They enabled farmers to concentrate on production and relieved their headaches about marketing but they must bear some of the responsibility for the subsequent neglect of marketing by farmers themselves. The Milk Marketing Board is by far the best known and most influential example, and it went from strength to strength, until recently liquidated to conform with the rules of the European Union.

The advent of war brought the administration of farm policy through the County War Agricultural Executive Committees. This entailed of necessity a very 'hands on' approach, and the progress of every farm was monitored right down to parish level, field by field. Writing of these days after the war, Dr William Davies, the well known grassland specialist, makes several interesting observations. 'One of the most encouraging features of our wartime agriculture was the friendship which has grown up between the technician and the farmer. This friendship is bound to be of immense economic consequence, and as the world settles down to its peacetime economics, the value of the technician to the farmer will steadily increase... The lead we gained in agricultural science and particularly in grassland and crop production during the 1920-40 period made us far less vulnerable than we otherwise would have been during the course of the Second World War. Had the technicians and farmers of this country not put into practice the result of their researches, we may not have held out on the food front in 1942-3. Much as our accumulated knowledge is, we are only on the threshold of greater things.'

The other notable feature of this wartime administration was the involvement of farmers themselves both at county and local level. They, supported or prompted by their executive officers, decided what should be done and when. In the case of dispute over acreage to be ploughed, it was a farmer from the District Committee who would walk the field with the owner or tenant. This administration put a premium on the maintenance of good relationships, but it certainly eliminated complaints of regulation by a distant bureaucracy. The classification of farms into Grades A, B, and C could be controversial but it was all documented on paper in a way which could not be fudged under challenge.

My own experience as a very junior employee of the Essex WAEC convinced me of the power of a united farming industry. Essex was, I believe, one of the largest of all the county committees, and it laid a particular emphasis on technical development. It has to be admitted that its growth involved the development of a certain bureaucratic structure, but it was run by farmers of powerful and highly individualistic character. Under the pressure of war, once decisions were made, things got done with speed and without question. Hundreds of acres of derelict land were cleared of thorn bushes, ploughed and farmed by the committee, while massive drainage operations were pursued without thought for anything but the urgent needs of food production. Extra labour was supplied to all who needed it through the Women's Land Army, and all the stops were pulled out to produce a rising crescendo.

My own duties included soil sampling and analysis as a basis for cropping programmes, and the sharing out of limited fertilisers. Essex was, I think, unique in having a rationing system for the lime and chalk needed to correct soil acidity. This was based not on any shortage of materials but rather to encourage people to use lime where it was needed. The theory was that if it was on permit it might be more valued psychologically, and those who had never bothered with having their soils tested would be more likely to take action. I was therefore empowered to write permits without any restriction on quantity, and there is no doubt that it stimulated conviction on the need to deal with soil acidity. Of course not all the administration was such plain sailing, and I was soon up against the perennial conundrum of whether one should bend the rules for deserving cases. A farm improvement might seem highly justified but still fail to satisfy all the criteria for a subsidy or for the release of scarce materials. My sympathies were instinctively with the farmer, and it was sometimes difficult to arrive at an objective assessment of what was right. Such experiences tended to convince me that I was not cut out to be an administrator, and reinforced the conviction already formed to farm on my own account after the war.

Administrative work, however, happily came second to technical development, and farmer discussion groups were actively promoted, as far as possible, with a group in each local district. These covered a wide variety of topics, and were the basic thrust in opening up the potential for progress. J C Leslie, the Chief Executive Officer and architect of WAEC programmes, was a man of big ideas, though perhaps on occasion rather too grand. R N Sadler, his successor, was more down-to-earth, and was not above sharing with us his own battles when first out of college. Occasionally, feeling utterly rejected and his advice unwanted, he would resort to Chelmsford Market, and seek comfort from huddling among the cattle. This provided some encouragement on the, fortunately, fairly rare occasions when it was clear that those I was dealing with thought I would be much better employed in one of the armed services. It is hard to imagine today that one could wish the Government to give a compulsory directive rather than leave it to individual decision. But it may have been a challenge that needed to be accepted. In any case, Sadler's own identification was with the familiar predicament of the newly qualified going out to meet men of far greater experience.

There is little question that the farmer's role in wartime did much to stimulate the development of the NFU (National Farmers Union). I remember, about this time, attending an Essex NFU Annual General Meeting addressed by James Turner (later Lord

Netherthorpe). He must have spoken for well over an hour setting out his vision for agriculture, but no-one became restless. He was already establishing an ascendancy over the Union which was to last for fifteen years, and which soon led to the establishment of the IFAP (International Federation of Agricultural Producers) in London in 1946, and the 1947 Agriculture Act enacted by that most popular of Agriculture Ministers, Labour's Tom Williams. The preamble of an early IFAP Conference (*IFAP Handbook*, Washington, 1952) describes the background.

> The idea of a world federation of farmers was spreading in the spring of 1945. A delegation from the NFU of England and Wales, fired with the idea, toured the British Commonwealth nations, United States and several other countries. The delegation met an enthusiastic reception to its scheme... On its return to England, the delegation sent invitations to attend an organisational meeting in London to all members of the United Nations who had a farm organisation. It was the first world wide conference of farmers, and thirty one nations were represented as delegates and observers at the meeting.

I was present at the founding of the IFAP in London, as were more experienced observers of the farming scene such as John Cherrington and Rex Paterson. I was greatly stirred by the thoughts of what it might be able to achieve. That many of those hopes have been disappointed does not detract from its aims, or the achievements as a discussion forum with which it can be credited. It has helped to provide a platform for the farmer's voice, and if a meaningful consensus has been difficult to reach, it has belatedly established the notion that, if farm issues are under discussion, there should be a place for the direct representation of farmers' views. More recently, under the General Secretaryship of Jo Feingold (formerly Kenya NFU) it has also put considerable effort into helping the establishment of farmers' organisations and cooperatives in countries which lack them. But it has to be said that IFAP remains largely unrecognised and unsung by the grass-roots farmers in most countries. Farmers generally have continued to see themselves, at least until recently, as one step removed from developments on the world stage. Had IFAP been able to articulate a united purpose for farmers, there is no doubt it would have had much greater impact.

Such a purpose had been for me one of the great preoccupations of the war years. Like many others, my father had spoken very little of his experiences in the First World War, but I hardly doubted that he felt a better future to be still possible. The increasing shadow of the Second World War during my later years at school made it seem something to be avoided at all costs. But when it became clear that this was not to be, it was obvious that winning the war had to be linked with a plan for an effective peace.

In the event, of course, such hopes were compromised by the Iron Curtain which divided Europe, and the continuing challenge of the Communist Empire. The declaration of war, to which I listened on the radio, proclaimed our intention to defend Poland. It was eventually undermined by the settlement at Yalta which left her at the mercy of the communists. Ideals seemed again to have fallen victim to realities, but I had learnt in the intervening years that the courage and conviction of ordinary people could fuel decisions which resulted in change. However small my influence might be, I could no longer accept that I was powerless to contribute.

Moreover the reality of the class divide on which communism had built seemed a particular challenge to one born into a landowning family. I can remember at an early age being occasionally troubled in spirit when addressed by one of my father's estate workers as 'Young Squire'. I didn't at the time stop to analyse the whys and wherefores. Nor did it particularly occur to me that we lived in an enormous mansion. I simply wondered vaguely why most of my school friends lived in such small houses!

All the same, I was glad to start work on a farm away from home, where my background was not known, and I felt valued for what I did rather than for any social position. It was a satisfaction which continued throughout the war years, and nourished the conviction that peace-time would see the dismantling of many social barriers. However, it was some years later still that I came to understand trade unionism and warm to the brotherhood of workers worldwide.

Meanwhile the 1947 Act, with its cast-iron guarantees to take all the food that farmers could produce, gave much-needed stability to post-war development. One forgets so quickly that some rationing actually continued into the 1950s, and that it was only much later that abundance became taken for granted. It was also not immediately apparent to everyone that Britain's pre-eminence in the industrial revolution had run its course, and that imports of cheap food would never again be a viable option, if they were seen as an alternative to an efficient and prosperous home agriculture. Thoughts flew to the basics of recovery rather than the longer-term future, and there was little awareness of what was happening in the rest of Europe.

The CAP (Common Agricultural Policy) gave the farming of the six European Community countries a considerable fillip in the sixties. In the space of ten years, a serious food shortage was turned into surplus in most commodities. Even in Britain, the concept of Standard Quantities, introduced when Christopher Soames was Minister of Agriculture, sought to limit the open-ended guarantee. By the time Britain joined the European Union, the CAP was already ripe for reform, but the 'unanimity' rule prevented any change that was not unanimously endorsed. That led to the patching up or adaptation of the existing structure, with the increasing surpluses that became all too familiar. Perhaps it has served to delay change until the need to conceive it on a world basis has become almost irresistible. What may not be so clear is the weighting to be given to the historical forces now at work and whether, in Dr Schumacher's striking phrase, 'economics can be made to work as if people really mattered'.

In farming, people have always mattered. It was fashionable at one time to point out that the advantage farming had in industrial relations was that the numbers employed were not large, and all had a direct relationship with the boss. But against that must be set the story of the Tolpuddle Martyrs, still honoured as pioneers of Trade Unionism in Britain. The first farm workers' union, founded under the leadership of Warwickshire's Joseph Arch in 1872, met bitter opposition. Karl Marx wrote, 'The great event here is the awakening of the agricultural labourers'. The preacher C H Spurgeon declared it 'The best news I have heard next to the Gospel'. Some twenty years later, Norfolk became the focal point of progress, and the union there, with painstaking and plodding work, built itself into a national organisation. 'I have done all kinds of things to settle disputes,' wrote one organiser, 'sometimes drawn "shorts" and sometimes spun a coin'. The same organiser remembered the time when, on his way through Lancashire, he cycled by a lonely farmstead to see a man standing alone at the gate in great distress. It seemed his three men had gone to market, and during their absence a valuable cow had been taken ill. The organiser got off his bike and went to have a look at the cow. He then got a horn, put on the farmer's wife's apron and gave the cow medicine. The farmer looked at him.

'Who are you?' he asked.

'I'm a labour organiser,' was the reply. 'Is it you that puts men into the union?'

The organiser nodded. 'I'm him.'

The farmer put out his hand: 'Well, put my three in and I'll pay for them,' he said (NUAW Official History).

This, however, was very much against the general run of experience. A later turning point came with the farm workers' strike of 1922, which was followed by the setting up of a Wages Board in 1924, the life of which has recently been prolonged by the unanimous wish of the industry in the face of a Government proposal for the abolition of all such arrangements. Certainly that strike marked the beginning of a regular dialogue with the NFU and, under the Presidency of Edwin Gooch, the NUAW (National Union of

Agricultural Workers) became a respected body with an active role in a wide variety of issues affecting the development of agriculture. Edwin Gooch was a blacksmith's son from Wymondham in Norfolk who was associated as a young man with the farm workers' struggle, though he himself became a journalist. Later he became Labour MP for North Norfolk and, as a friend of Peter Howard, was sometimes a visitor to the latter's farm in Suffolk.

I mention this because in the years immediately after the war I worked for Peter Howard on his farm near Lavenham, and it made a decisive impact on my thinking and living. Peter was a dynamic character who led from the front and, inspired by his contact with Moral Re-Armament, was determined that his farm become a pattern of what God meant it to be. This included profitability and technical excellence but, above everything, it represented a challenge to the motivation of all who worked with him. He was unsparingly honest about himself, and for that reason was surprisingly sensitive to all that goes on deep inside people. When he first came back to run the farm himself, rather than through a manager, he had just left a highly paid job with the Beaverbrook newspapers. He was a very successful, nationally-known journalist, but acutely aware of his ignorance about farming. From the start he made it clear that he wanted to learn from the local people who had the experience, and it was not long before Tom Beeton, the tractor driver, was moved to be honest with him about equipment and materials that he had stolen for his own use. It was the foundation of an enduring friendship, and Tom became a rock on which the daily working of the farm was founded. For Tom made the life of the farm one with his own life, entering into the spirit of all that went on including the annual Horkeys (harvest suppers) traditional in Suffolk. While these included songs, music or recitations, they also gave a platform to those with experiences of change in their own lives to share, which linked with a vision for the post-war world. They became unique gatherings where a cross-section of the neighbourhood met with frequent guests from many different countries, a preview of Peter's future years at the forefront of the expansion of Moral Re-Armament.

For me personally, there was a challenge to the slipshod and easy-going approach to things and people which often spoilt my work. I remember one occasion when I was exercising the bull, and two rather dubious looking characters turned up to buy old sacks. I broke off long enough to do a deal with them but, with no-one else around to lend a hand, I failed to supervise the loading of the sacks. This resulted in them taking some top quality seed sacks from the firm of Pertwee, which were not a part of the deal. Peter left me in no doubt of his feelings on the matter when he returned. Finally a belated phone call to try and redress the wrong revealed only that they were known to the Police and it was too late to recover the booty! But if he could be fierce in his criticisms, Peter was also both generous and convincing in his encouragement. As a student, I had first gone to Hill Farm to help with the harvest in 1941, and the following winter Peter wrote to me, 'I was joyful to get your letter, it is a real encouragement and help to all of us here to know that a person with your specialised knowledge, which none of us have, is taking an interest in and responsibility for the place... There are many points which I would much like to discuss with you, Pat, and the sooner the better as Spring sowing is coming on.' This came to a comparatively immature student who did not have half as much to offer as Peter implied, but who was passionately keen to get involved. What I had to learn was not to be buffeted by the powerful personalities of others, but to go back to the prompting of my own conscience and God's word to me in my own heart. Only then could I be truly free of what other people thought, and able to forge friendships which owed nothing to the search for approval. It is not an easily digested lesson, but it has been for me a crucial one.

Later Peter encouraged me to write and to express ideas on paper, joking on one occasion that I suffered from 'mental diarrhoea and verbal constipation'. He was always fun to be with, as wholehearted in play as at work, and I well remember, when playing tag with the children, how he managed to evade my best efforts. He would let me get within feet of him, and then dance and dodge away as nimble as someone half his size. I don't believe I ever managed to touch him, and it was all the more remarkable since he had a lame leg which was no more than a thin pillar of bone. He has described how on the international rugby field he would wrap a bandage or puttee round it inside his stocking to make it look more normal and allay any anxiety among the selectors. On one occasion he forgot his bandage, and stuffed a towel round his leg before moving out on to the field. Then at one point he made a major break down the field, while the towel came undone and was flapping at his heels like a terrier, much to the crowd's amusement and his own mortification.

Peter Howard went on to become a world figure, known to thousands in many countries. Always a man of action, he reached an even wider audience through his writing. He spent himself with a wholeheartedness and urgency that was awesome. Many of his plays and books were written in the early hours of the morning before a day busy with people and events. He told me once that he used to think that if he had had more space to write he might have produced something of greater literary merit. But latterly he had come to doubt the truth of this. Whatever its literary merit, his writing gripped hearts and minds. It is a legacy which will be finally evaluated in the new century. For he died suddenly of a virus infection in 1965 at the age of fifty-six.

In the 24 years that I knew him, it was a revelation to see a dynamic and dominant personality transforming into a man led by God. The power and love of God became central to his living in a way which seemed increasingly to take him beyond the purely charismatic. It prompted Claudius Petit, a Minister in a number of post-war French Governments, to declare 'C'est un génie'. This was in 1955, when Claudius Petit took part in a Moral Re-Armament initiative which was dubbed the World Mission. Peter Howard's musical play, *The Vanishing Island*, was the centrepiece of the presentation. It was described by its author as, '"not the story of any one country. It is the story of every country and every human heart in the world today". For three months, 244 people of 28 nationalities visited 18 countries on four continents. In 11 countries they were government guests' (*Frank Buchman – A Life*, Garth Lean). Some people saw *The Vanishing Island* only as representing the gulf between the communist and non-communist world. But its journey round the world was sustained by a trained force of people who understood that the future would have to be shaped by concepts beyond capitalism and communism as we knew them. That is why its prophetic message still needs to be digested in the different context of today. For too few at the time recognised the significance of this surprising mobilisation.

Through all the outreach of his later years, the strand of Peter's farming interest ran deep and true. Not only did he keep a close correspondence with his farm manager, but his love of the land was always part of his essential definition of Britain and the service of his life. On the steps of St Martin's in the Fields, after the memorial service for him, I met Lord Netherthorpe after a gap of several years. He spoke of how moving he had found the service and the address by the Right Hon. Quintin Hogg (Lord Hailsham). Later he wrote, 'Peter will be sorely missed'. Certainly the deep inward sorrow I felt myself hardened into a decision to try and stick with the world task to which he had been dedicated. In farming terms, it meant discovering how the farming way of life could remain relevant, and contribute something vital to a rapidly changing world. Farmers have always seen themselves as an essential part of national life, but we have not always felt so confident in the face of modern developments which sometimes threaten to shape our lives rather than serve our purposes.

Probably that is a concern of many, and I do not wish to dwell unduly on my own experience, except in so far as it illustrates the process by which someone takes on a greater aim in life than simply making a living. For me, that vision began with meeting Moral Re-Armament, and was stimulated working with Peter Howard. For those who have never heard of Moral Re-Armament, the subject can be pursued through the notes at the back of this book. But the revelation which particularly hit me, was the existence of a path which could serve the whole of humanity on its forward march to a new future. For Moral Re-Armament is not an organisation with a list of members, and a particular way of doing things. It includes people of all religions and of no religion, and it calls on people to begin their contribution to change in the world by change in themselves.

Although brought up in the Anglican Church, I have to confess that I had never measured my life in any concrete detail against the absolute nature of Christ's standards of honesty, purity, unselfishness and love. It was for that reason, perhaps, that my faith had dwindled almost to the point of disappearance. But an even greater step was to begin to listen to the voice of God in my heart, that inner voice which is instantly available to anyone ready to make a serious experiment. I have no doubt that the decision to take time to listen in this way daily has been the most important of my life. It has opened my eyes to many things of which I had previously been unaware. Peoples and nations show a great diversity, but human nature remains the same all over the world. We are all conversant with its weaknesses, but Pope John Paul II has suggested that 'Man does not cease to be great, not even in his weakness'. Those who want the truth badly enough will be led to it from whatever quarter they approach.

Against this background, the shock of Peter Howard's death was all the greater because his work, in human terms, seemed so unfinished. As the leader of a world work in succession to Dr Frank Buchman, its initiator, he was inundated by those who sought his counsel. He told me that he expected to find, for everyone he met, a vision of the person God meant them to be. But he did not expect to know what they ought to be doing or where they ought to work. Perhaps too many human expectations which should have been addressed elsewhere were unloaded on him. Certainly it was not easy to take up the full dimension of the battle he had waged. Yet throughout my life in farming I have been sustained by the vision discovered at this time, however imperfectly pursued. It has to do with a sense of purpose inherent from man's earliest history, but which needs the constant accumulation of fresh insights through succeeding years. That is the spiritual challenge in the unparalleled opportunities which a growing number are granted today. So a new unity of purpose may only take shape as we understand the need not to possess the truth, but to be possessed by it. It is part of a learning process which knows no end and, in that sense, like farming, goes on for ever.

Chapter 4
Science and Progress

A major focus of this learning process today is the onward march of science. Even in the 1930s, scientists were beginning to realise that a commitment to their chosen subject involved wider considerations.

'At first I had intended to write about the land in its agricultural implications only. Today, however, that is not enough, for the land must be considered in relation to the nation as a whole.' Thus wrote Sir George Stapledon in the preface to his book, *The Land – Now and Tomorrow*, published in 1935. A pioneer of improved grassland, he was a specialist whose vision always extended way beyond his own subject. So he was well placed to pose questions about the nature of progress. For the speed with which scientific knowledge has accelerated is a commonplace. It has gained an unstopable momentum. Yet there are growing question marks over the use which we make of our knowledge.

Stapledon, in the course of his book, voices his unease at the excessive specialisation towards which science and, indeed, farming itself seemed to be heading. 'The unexpected is the only certainty in a world seething with unrest, and in an age driven headlong, it knows not in what direction, by the discoveries of science... The tendency today is still to staff and administer even applied research on the basis of the sciences and subjects rather than on the basis of problems.' He then makes the point that overlapping may not be something to be avoided at all costs. 'It is bad for a man and for an institution to feel in sole possession of a problem – every problem is the property of mankind.'

If such observations had been heeded, we might have avoided some of the pitfalls of excessive specialisation, which led to the well-known definition of an expert as someone who knows more and more about less and less. It is also striking that most of the prominent agricultural scientists whose names became household words at this time, were men of notable common sense and a good measure of humility. This did not mean that they were always right but it ensured that they did not stray very far from the values on which progress depends. Science deals with facts and how things happen, but applied research means taking decisions on how such knowledge should be used in practical affairs.

Looking back on the days when I was a junior technical officer with the Essex War Agricultural Committee, I remember an occasion when a speaker scheduled to give a talk on cereal diseases had to cry off at short notice. I decided to let the meeting go ahead and to give the talk myself. It went off without much comment, and without my being floored in question time. I was gratified when my boss, Ben Harvey, told me later that I had done myself a bit of good locally by giving the talk myself. But looking back with hindsight, it is surprising to realise that it was possible in the space of a few hours to brush up on most of what was then known about cereal diseases in practical terms. I was not particularly good at plant pathology as a student but I had no difficulty in refreshing my memory for an evening.

Nevertheless, the momentum that science has developed totally alters the picture today. So it is worth remembering some of the issues raised when the first atomic bombs were dropped on Japan at the end of the war. They are issues both of conscience and of the principles of scientific enquiry. Clearly, in the context of its destructive potential, the only justification for using the bomb was to bring the war to a rapid end.

President Truman made that unenviable decision, and it did end the war. At the same time, the terrible sickness engendered by radiation was not foreseen in all its stark horror, and that has left a painful legacy through the years. It may possibly be true that the deterrent effect of the bomb owed something to that terrible experience but, while deterrence may have worked for the times we have lived through, it has nothing to offer for the future.

The Hiroshima Memorial carries a commitment to live differently for today, and it becomes more poignant with the passage of the years. For science pursues its headlong road simply because it must always be an open-ended pursuit of knowledge. It is the endless enquiry into how things work in the world we live in, and having set out in pursuit of it, we cannot call a halt. But we still have to address the questions 'why?' and 'to what purpose?' Many had supposed that science could answer them. It was still a time when science was inclined to be credited with its own peculiar wisdom and to be thought thereby, *ipso facto*, a source of leadership in the world. When it comes to weapons of mass destruction, it is not difficult to find a big majority in favour of pursuing more creative aims. At the same time there is a reaction to atomic physics which owes more to fear than to reason. The difficulties of ensuring safety are real enough, even if Chernobyl only happened in the face of wilful and deliberate neglect of the rules. Furthermore, the disposal of radioactive waste has still to find a satisfactory answer. Perhaps the biggest mistake has been the pressure to rush things forward. A hope was nourished that atomic energy might be a quick way out of our difficulties. More truthfully it is a door opened on yet unfulfilled possibilities, but it is a pity that warnings against its misuse should be linked in the public mind to what are perceived as inevitable dangers. There is no reason why Atomic energy should not in the end prove beneficial.

In agriculture, it is the chemical industry which has so far borne the brunt of the attack against the misuse of science. *Silent Spring* by Rachel Carson put down a marker. It is not difficult to point out mistakes such as the use of Dieldrin, which proved far more persistent than had been expected. It was, of course, its persistence which recommended it for sheep dips when one could be reasonably sure that a single dip would see off flies for the whole period of major risk. Many, myself included, were sorry to see it go for this reason, but there is no disputing that it was a right decision. Other chemicals have been withdrawn after initial approval, and it is this as much as anything which leads to negative publicity and undermines trust. But it is a pity that 'chemical' farming has become confused in the public mind with the idea that it is inherently unnatural. It is after all the function of plants to turn inorganic chemicals into organic chemicals, and we are learning all the time what is and is not helpful to this process. With pesticides, it is rather more straightforward, as it is immediately apparent that they may kill not only pests but their natural predators too; and there has already been a marked change in attitude to their use.

However, the controversies lying ahead are going to centre particularly on biological science, the science of life itself. Only today is farming beginning to bump up against ethical considerations in such developments and, so far as livestock are concerned, many of the issues are shared with the field of human medicine. Indeed it is often a matter of comment in Britain that the welfare of animals sometimes arouses fiercer emotions than the welfare of human beings. Here again, each new breakthrough in research is apt to be trumpeted as the instant road to all sorts of spectacular change. But it would be more helpful if we discussed and defined the kind of changes which could be desirable, while the scientists put in the further years of research needed to bring techniques to fruition.

In view of the fact that scientific advances are going to be increasingly under public scrutiny, it is important to realise that the mere acquisition of knowledge does not determine the way knowledge will be used. It is still instructive to read the proceedings of the Lenin Academy of Agricultural Sciences in 1948, when communist ideology was perhaps at its zenith. Professor T D Lysenko, then President of the Academy, was engaged in fierce controversy with geneticists who accepted the orthodox view of heredity. Lysenko propounded the Marxist theory that acquired characters could be inherited, and therefore did not depend on chromosomes or hereditary substance, but resulted from changes in the living body itself. It was formulated by I V Michurin, whose theme was, 'We cannot wait for favours from Nature, we must wrest them from her'.

This led Lysenko to declare, 'The materialist theory of the evolution of living nature necessarily presupposes the recognition of hereditary transmission of individual characteristics acquired by the organism under definite conditions of life: it is unthinkable, without recognition of the inheritance of acquired characters'. The ramifications of this controversy were underlined by another speaker, who said it was time to break the corrupting influence of bourgeois science on other specialities, notably philosophy. He called on philosophers to develop and express the philosophical depth of Lysenko's science. By the end of the conference, the Marxist position on the situation in biological science was established, as one after another of the dissenting geneticists recanted on their previous speeches. One declared, 'The speech I made the day before yesterday at a time when the Central Committee of the Party had drawn a dividing line between the two trends in biological science, was unworthy of a member of the Communist Party and of a Soviet scientist'. Only a lone voice stuck to the point: 'The truth, of course, will always remain the truth, and it will triumph in the end'. Perhaps the remarkable thing is that such a comment still appeared in the official record (*Proceedings of the Lenin Academy of Agricultural Sciences*, Session July 31-August 7, 1948).

This may seem old history now, but current disputes also can easily turn into a struggle about who's right rather than what's right. For me, it has always seemed that one of the first lessons of farming is that two and two do not always make four. This is not to deny the mathematical exactitude of scientific fact but to underline the infinite variations which life itself brings to any equations. Genetic variability is almost endless, and makes breeding an immensely complicated proceeding. The Russians under Lysenko had even come to the point where they denied the value of progeny testing. Small wonder that they were unable to make a creative contribution to collective farming. Yet, while computers are no better than their operators, they have immensely eased the task of evaluating complex data. It always seems a little unreal to my untutored mind, to compete for growing the biggest crop of wheat on computer, but the value of the tool is well established!

All the same, the answers that come out are no better than the data supplied. So it is for this reason that I believe science should jealously guard the long term perspective and that scientists should take responsibility for their own judgements on commercial exploitation. When progesterone sponges were first being used for synchronised and out-of-season breeding in ewes, we were invited to take part in a trial. By the time our results and observations were sent in, the product had already been launched commercially, and was being promoted with vigour. So no acknowledgement was made of our results, and no reply offered on one or two questions posed. I am not saying that there may not have been ample evidence in favour of going ahead before our contribution was completed, simply that there was a striking evaporation of interest in further scientific enquiry once the product was licensed and approved. Trials are diligently pursued in order to obtain a licence, but that is rarely the end of the story. Commercial development usually requires the organisation of some extension work to ensure that the product is used correctly, but too often it does not include an interest in the byways of knowledge or even the possible longer-term consequences. This attitude may sometimes be justified on economic grounds by those who emphasise the enormous cost of launching a new product, but it cannot be justified scientifically.

Further conflicts are also possible when the public refuses to accept something that has been approved by the scientists. One example is over the use of growth hormones in beef production. Their use has been banned in the European Union despite a scientific committee having delivered a verdict in their favour. As a result, many Americans appear to believe that the ban is simply a subterfuge to prevent them exporting to Europe. In this case the scientists are convinced that, with a necessary withdrawal period being observed, there is not the slightest danger to human health. The customers, on the other hand, are not sure that they want the growth of beef animals stimulated by scientific intervention, and call for meat without the use of additives.

The scientist who regards himself as the arbiter of truth may have difficulty in coming to terms with this situation. But, like the farmer, he has to accept that the customer is always right and, if he wants to alter a position he has to do it by persuasion. In a democratic society, the only course open is for the scientist to improve the layman's understanding by clarifying the technical issues. In this, the professional press plays a vital role and has an impressive record. Too often on the other hand, the popular press starts by going over the top, as in the case of BSE (Bovine Spongiform Encephalopathy) in cattle or Salmonella in poultry. The result is a catastrophic drop in the market, which may not return to normal for a year or even longer. Usually the scare tends to be soon forgotten, except by those whose livelihoods have suffered.

Bridging such differences is to a very great extent a matter of learning to deal with human nature, our own and other people's! I can well remember the confrontation between Dr William Davies, the grassland specialist, and Dr Reg Preston, then at the Rowett Research Institute, when the latter first unveiled his work on Barley Beef. Preston was speaking at a Farmers Club meeting entitled, 'Four Ways to Beef', held in December 1961. He gave a very able account of his work, and concluded his presentation with the assertion that, 'The basis of a new truly intensive system of beef production has been formulated. The next few years will decide the extent to which these ideas have application in the business of making a profit from beef cattle.' Davies's reactions were not, I think, entirely aroused by the merits or otherwise of the case presented. He felt that cattle were essentially grassland animals, and that the emphasis on fattening them with barley was in the long term a kind of heresy, a feeling no doubt fuelled by Preston's brashness and youth. He proceeded to criticise Preston for overestimating the cost of starch equivalent from grass in winter feeding, and for encroaching on the domain of the practical farmer, for which he had no qualification. It was the latter comment which got under Preston's skin, because he was a farmer's son with plenty of practical experience at a tender age. Although I am sure the record in the *Farmers' Club Journal* is impeccable, it does nothing to convey the strong feelings aroused in both men! The moment passed, but it was a classic confrontation between the new and the old, the iconoclast and the traditionalist.

Looking back, it is interesting to note Preston's closing remarks in his reply to Davies. 'Dr Davies mentioned resources in agriculture. We are aware of the world situation. At the same time, the economists tell us that it should not be long before we shall find resources being taken out of agriculture, despite international shortages: resources in terms of farmers, land, scientists and so on. But that is not my angle.' Since then, we have seen the rise of vegetarian and famine-conscious opinion against beef as an inefficient use of land resources. It is a criticism often made without thought to the natural grasslands of the world and how they can best be utilised. But so far as it concerns barley beef, the fact has to be faced that feed grain gravitates to the available markets. If it is needed to combat famine or malnutrition, it still has to be bought in the market, otherwise it will not be grown. So barley beef has held its share of the market where grain prices have justified it, while the part played by the length of fibre in the diets of ruminants has become better understood. It is more a question of options than basic policy.

'Practice with Science' has been the motto which has sustained the Royal Agricultural Society of England for 150 years, and the bond between farmer and scientist is a close one. In my own brief experience on the scientific side of the fence, I can remember what pleasure it gave to conduct a trial which actually produced a copy-book result. In this case it was a 1943 trial of the combine drilling of spring barley and superphosphate on highly phosphate-deficient land. The plots showed clearly that 1.5 hundredweight (cwt) of superphosphate drilled beside the seed was more effective than 3 cwt broadcast, thus making the case both for the combine drill and for economy in the use of fertiliser. It was important to remember that this was a trial on phosphate-deficient land, because some were inclined to run away with the idea that combine drilling was necessarily superior in all circumstances. In fact such differences do not show up in soils well supplied with phosphate. But while the experiment had to be quantified in terms of actual yield, the striking thing was that the results were unmistakably visible to everyone visiting the site.

When the facts are less clearly established, there is even more to be gained from working together, and the search for answers can be shared without any guarantee that they will lead to commercial profit. I can remember being quite surprised during the investigations into forward creep grazing of lambs that our experience on the optimum number of paddocks to use was received as seriously helpful by the researchers at Hurley. But the net result of the work was to establish that while it was possible to improve productivity per acre, the game was probably not worth the candle in most circumstances. More general measures have now been defined for rotational grazing and the overall reduction of worm burdens, which have been widely accepted into practice. But one experience leads to another, and they are all part of building up a comprehensive picture.

Some years later I had occasion to write to the Weed Research Organisation on the subject of CDA (Controlled Droplet Application) spraying. I received an excellent and thoughtful letter from George Cussans, one of the staff, setting out his view of the points at issue. This covered the possibility of lower dose rates and smaller quantities of water, while pointing out the lack of any depth of evidence on the exact validity of such proposals. In summing up, he suggested that basically it was a choice between sticking in the mainstream of tested experience or risking participation at the frontiers of knowledge where experience had to be bought before the way could be clearly marked out. Needless to say, I was usually inclined to try out something new, though Mike Finch, our tractor driver, sometimes teased me for being too ready to experiment and embark on trials.

Incidentally, one of the early pioneers of CDA in spraying was the firm of Micron in Bromyard, founded and led by Edward Bals. Their approach had the merit of simplicity but it was also both economical and effective. The result has been that the bulk of their business has been done with developing countries, and it is a pity that much development has had to be made in the face of opposition or indifference from the big chemical companies. This arose from the fact that, while CDA might widen the application of chemicals, it would be more likely to reduce gross consumption. It could be said that Micron is a fine example of Schumacher's dictum that 'small is beautiful'. Edward was preoccupied with the aim of directing the chemical efficiently to where it was needed, using the smallest quantity necessary and eliminating drift. He welcomed the participation of all concerned to this end, and included in it the health and safety of sprayer operators in the developing countries. He was committed to doing a good practical job for the farmers' benefit.

Whatever path is chosen, it is clear that sooner or later a fresh area of middle ground is established. New ideas are either incorporated into practice or they fall by the wayside, occasionally to be revived or even rediscovered some years later. But although this may be seen as the established path of progress, it does not always run smoothly. All the same, it will be a sad day if farmers come to feel they can no longer afford to experiment, and the zest for study and enquiry is cut off by the accountant's bottom line. Not that being cost effective is always a negative. It can often be instrumental in promoting the cause of simplicity against excessive complication.

Just such an example can be detected in the current moves to look at how far inputs can be reduced without a major effect on output. This is promptly labelled less intensive farming, but it is worth remembering that the most intensively cultivated land in the kingdom is in our gardens and allotments. There is nothing wrong with intensive farming, only with the upsets which occur through pursuing an unbalanced system. Oliver Walston's comparisons of wheat growing costs in different countries illustrate the point. (*Farmers Weekly*, November 1992). His yields are miles ahead of the Americas or Australia, but his inputs also leave him with the most costly grain per ton. Yet we cannot, even in East Anglia, afford to farm extensively, because our land is so limited. The only possible approach is to see how much can be trimmed from inputs while still improving rather than impairing the gross margin. However, there must always be the added rider that soil fertility be maintained.

Such an approach may seem straightforward to the lay mind, but there are many factors to be examined. Crop rotations, cultivations, the incidence of disease and pests, even the introduction of live-stock, may all enter into the equation, and need evaluating over a number of years. Researchers such as Dr Vic Jordan at Long Ashton are already at work and beginning to feed back early experiences. While in the USA such initiatives are dubbed Alternative Agriculture and have already been the subject of an official report by a committee of the Board of Agriculture (National Research Council).

The US Board makes the point that 'interest in Alternative Farming Systems is often motivated by a desire to reduce health and environmental hazards, and a commitment to natural resource stewardship. But the most important criterion for many farmers considering a change in farming practices is the likely economic outcome. Wide adoption of alternative farming methods requires that they be at least as profitable as conventional methods, or have significant non-monetary advantages, such as preservation of rapidly deteriorating soil or water resources.' Nothing can be described as entirely new in any of these approaches. Rather, it is the realisation that there are many more choices than is sometimes realised when following the well-worn tracks. For science is constantly enlarging these choices. In such circumstances, farming is very much the art of orchestrating the right overall approach. Specialisation may still have its place but tunnel-vision can be fatal.

Lord Plumb put the case for more research rather than less in a speech at Cirencester in December 1994.

> The challenge, therefore, is adequately to fund agricultural development and productivity improvement, which is unwisely being reduced in both developed and developing countries.
>
> There is at least a twenty-year lag between initiating strategic research and significant increases of production in areas of need.
>
> Twenty years from now there will be 2 billion more people to feed, and most will be in developing countries' cities.
>
> Not to recognise the challenge, and increase efforts, is bad enough, but it is much worse to allow existing research capacity to erode, particularly when biotechnology can produce such unprecedented advance at an undreamed-of pace.

His points were uppermost in my mind as I listened to a biotechnologist describe his experiences at the International Farmers Dialogue held in January 1995 at Caux, Switzerland. Dr Ian Robertson, of the University of Zimbabwe, outlined the work he had begun in potatoes by introducing a gene resistant to the leaf roll virus, a major brake on crop yields locally. As a Scottish TV programme recorded, he had done this despite a limited budget, by using empty peanut butter jars collected for the laboratory by schoolchildren, cotton wool as a cheap substitute for imported agar, and a modified airgun as a substitute for the extremely expensive gene gun normally used. The low-tech stage of this programme has now been completed and, through tissue culture, clean, virus-free potatoes are now in the fields of both communal and commercial farmers, eliminating the bottleneck of elite seed shortage. Similar work with cassava has recently delivered plants to two hundred and sixty five very poor Mozambican farmers through a German aid programme. Robertson estimates that such virus-free plants will double the yields of potatoes and triple the yields of cassava. He is now working on the next stage, which is to incorporate the genes in the make-up of the plant, so that resistant types can be bred.

Such dramatic progress is highly significant for African farmers, but this is not the usual route for commercially motivated science. Robertson has already been offered three times his present salary to work elsewhere, but he intends to stick with his vision for African farming. I am grateful for this but sorry that the benefits of science should generally go only to those with the money to exploit them. Intellectual property rights need to be sorted out in an equitable manner, but rather more honesty and clarity about the points at issue would be a help. Few farmers who have benefited from improved varieties would grudge the payment of royalties to the scientist who bred them. But there is something wrong when a scientist is encouraged to pursue his own initiatives in a situation where no great amount of money will be generated, but warned that if it becomes big business someone will be looking for up to 40% of the takings. It would also seem questionable that peasant farmers should be asked to pay royalties on the seed they save for their own use, the more so if the variety involved has been bred with the help of indigenous material freely gathered in the wild.

The answer to this situation is not immediately apparent, though it is clearly not enough to say that he who pays the piper calls the tune. Ethics are beginning to be seen as more necessary to business than has been popularly supposed. So perhaps there could be a meeting of minds between science and business. Certainly, if we are to meet the needs of a growing world population, science has to be at the service of the people. Many scientists would subscribe to the view that the new developments in biotechnology need to be in the hands of good people, that is to say people who are not simply interested in exploiting them for their own ends. Perhaps if the enormous benefits of scientific discovery are to be harvested as they should, science and philosophy will have to be reunited. That is perhaps a logical sequel to rejecting scientific materialism in favour of an open-ended pursuit of truth.

Chapter 5
Agriculture and the Environment

When it comes to a linkage between science and the environment, popular interest has perhaps already usurped the scientists' monopoly on interpreting the scene. We live in an age when interest in the environment is rising steadily, even among those whose links with agriculture have been cut long since. It is a development to be welcomed wholeheartedly, but it can easily lead to misconceptions and a diversion from fundamentals. G V Jacks and R O Whyte open their study of soil erosion round the world with such a fundamental. 'To gain control over the soil is the greatest achievement of which mankind is capable.' They then proceed to cite several civilisations whose decline and fall has been associated with massive soil erosion and the formation of desert, due to the pressure put on the soil by their expansion.

In their book, *The Rape of the Earth*, published before World War II, they outline the normal erosion found in nature, and the accelerated erosion caused by man.

> Erosion in Nature is a beneficial process without which the world would have died long ago. The same process, accelerated by human mismanagement, has become one of the most vicious and destructive forces that have ever been released by man. What is usually known as 'geological erosion' or 'denudation' is a universal phenomenon which, through thousands of years, has carved the earth into its present shape. Denudation is an early and important process in soil formation whereby the original rock material is continuously broken down and sorted out until it becomes suitable for colonisation by plants. Plants, by the binding effect of their roots, by the protection they afford against rain and wind and by the fertility which they impart to the soil,

bring denudation almost to a standstill... Nevertheless some slight denudation is always occurring. The earth is continuously discarding its old, worn out skin and renewing its living sheath of soil from the dead rock beneath.

They go on to make the point that, in Western Europe, agriculture has been a practice tending on the whole to enhance soil fertility. But soil fertility is connected more to soil stability than to the plant food supply, because even exhausted soils usually contain a supply of plant food. But exhausted soils are unstable because they lack organic matter, and what has been created over the long haul can be removed in the space of only a few decades. This process, of course, markedly reduces the water-holding capacity of the soil, and perceptions that dry weather is increasing can also be fostered by the fact that more rain is needed where fertility has decreased.

It is clear therefore that the most important question for our farming today is whether or not soil fertility is being maintained. Other environmental considerations may have their impact visually on the landscape, but are essentially secondary in fundamental terms. Hedges that owe their origins to the enclosures can be removed, and if necessary replaced elsewhere. Shelter belts can combine practical use with aesthetic considerations, while man-made constructions such as silos and windmills can always be removed. Their constructors will naturally hope for the maximum working life, but such constructions are not an irrevocable blot on the landscape.

Management practices, too, may be modified for the sake of appearances, save in the case of habitats which depend more on nature than on agriculture. Ancient woodland, wetlands and heath need protection from agriculture if they are to be preserved, while areas of hill or common grassland may need a careful adjustment of grazing intensity to maintain their particular balance. But it is unwise to argue from this that extensive livestock grazing is more suitable for maintaining soil fertility than intensive. In many

European situations the opposite will be true, and in any case it will depend on the farmer's overall strategy for the use of his land. Land in grass will generally be enhancing soil fertility, and this, in suitable situations, can be cashed in crops. But for land which is under continuous arable cultivation, different considerations come into play.

For the layman, it is worth noting the differences that can be observed between cultivating pronounced slopes on the chalk downs of the south and on the hills of Wales. On the downs, the soils are often not deep, but they have been kept in cereal growing because the price for grain has been tempting. In some cases, visible and catastrophic soil erosion has resulted. Opinions seem to vary about who should be held responsible for this but, to my mind, it is the farmer who must hold himself responsible. He cannot be led into bad farming just because he calculates it may be more profitable.

The Welsh hills, on the other hand, now have extremely stable soils and you frequently see slopes cultivated on which I, for one, would not care to drive a tractor, yet the soil remains stable. At the same time it has to he said, of course, that such slopes are not destined for regular arable cultivation.

Sheet erosion by water can also be a gradual process which is not always recognised until, over the years, the level at the bottom end of the field has visibly risen. This can easily be seen by its height against the fence. It may happen so gradually that the farmer is barely worried, but it should always be taken as the writing on the wall. Generally speaking, the British farmer is not erosion-conscious to the same extent as the American farmer, because he has not faced anything so dramatic as the prairie Dust Bowl in the thirties. So it was quite a surprise when an Indian farmer of great skill and expertise who was visiting, pressed on me the need to pay attention to contours in cultivations. Yet in the United States today, all farmers wishing to take part in programmes of price support must, as a condition of doing so, participate in measures for soil conservation.

Further afield, in South Africa for example, the acute issues of soil erosion have been obscured from the public mind by the long running battle over Apartheid. Yet in earlier days General Smuts could say, 'Erosion is the biggest problem confronting the country, bigger than any politics'. Uneducated farmers were blamed for not taking more notice of the danger, but life is not always that simple. The experience of Roland Kingwill, a farmer on the Karoo in the Eastern Cape Province, is illuminating. Roly was at that time a young farmer with a heavy mortgage on his land, who was struggling for economic viability by carrying the maximum number of sheep that he could. Yet it was clear enough that their heavy grazing was detrimental to his soil, and the growing number of gullies was a warning of worse to come. There came a moment when, as he describes it, he moved from the Christianity of a conventional churchgoer to the Christianity of obedience. When he asked God what He wanted of him and listened in silence, one of the first thoughts that came was, 'Reduce your numbers of livestock by one third'. It was a struggle for him to be ready to carry this out, but he did, and the benefit to the farm soon became visible. The Merino sheep began to cut a heavier fleece and the cattle carried more flesh than they had ever managed before. Roly became a pioneer of better grassland practice.

Not only that, he also built a school for the children on the farm and paid for a teacher, before the days when government was prepared to support such initiatives. Later the family sought to combat unemployment by promoting rural crafts and a co-operative business in woollen and leather goods. As Roly put it, the riches were of the spirit rather than in the bank balance, but he found life deeply satisfying, and contributed directly to inter-racial harmony.

Yet, while it didn't make him a rich man, it proved a viable way of farming and one with increasing rather than diminishing prospects. His sons today still aim for the farm to support as many workers as possible, rather than pursue the possible cost effectiveness of much-reduced labour. Their strategy is not one of blind faith, but of striving to grapple with the practical problems that bedevil South African society. So they continue to be pioneers of the moral and spiritual advances which will help carry South Africa into a new century. Then perhaps it may even be perceived again that there are more important things than politics! Or rather that daily life on a remote farm may have a profound effect on the political climate.

Be that as it may, it is a fair point that, where love is involved, only the best is good enough, and it is given from the heart rather than extracted by argument. So the key to a better environment may lie more in a change of heart than in simply campaigning for particular practices. This could also be relevant to the question of sustainable agriculture, where no easy definitions are available. Research needs to be well directed to throw light on the areas of real doubt, and criticisms of current practice need to avoid becoming prematurely ideological. Science is as much concerned with the pursuit of truth as philosophy is, and we are all, in varying degrees, seeking new roads ahead.

Already, some chickens are coming home to roost on issues like crop rotation and plant health, the breeding of varieties resistant to disease and a number of others. But to erect on this an argument that all influences towards extensification are bound to be benign, and all those towards intensification malign, is almost certainly unreasonable! Nature often shows itself capable of a good deal more than we are inclined to credit. But a great many judgements can only be made over a lengthy time-scale so that, when it comes to the monoculture of cereals or any other type of crop, the sustainability of yields over a farming lifetime is not conclusive evidence that the soil is not deteriorating. Experiments at Rothamsted, now in place for 150 years, come nearer to the kind of perspective that is needed.

It is interesting, looking back, that debates about organic farming in the early 1940s turned on whether or not the humus content of the soil was increasing or decreasing, and whether the farming system followed was maintaining the input of organic matter, either by farmyard manure or by green manuring. Chemical argument was confined to the use of fertilisers, which were and are a useful supplement of readily-available plant food. Assertions that they killed earthworms and poisoned the soil have not been substantiated. In the Rothamsted experiments, soils on which wheat has been grown continuously, some with nitrogen fertiliser and some without, but with nothing else, show a small advantage for the area receiving nitrogen, both in content of organic matter and the activity of micro-organisms. This has been presumed to be due to the larger quantity of plant residue being ploughed back where nitrogen was applied.

But the real issue in the long-term remains the question of soil structure, and it is worth all the concern that can be lavished on it. Both minimal cultivations and the wide variety of power harrows in use have increased the range of soil treatments open to us, but too often choices are made only in terms of economics or yield in the current crop. Although these are bound to be the first considerations, they are not the end of the story.

On the whole, however, we feel more at home with questions of immediate pollution and the nuts and bolts of putting it right. Obvious pollution such as the overflow of silage liquor or slurry can soon be dealt with, and could in most cases be avoided by better design. But estimates of the cost involved in putting a situation right need to be looked at very carefully, as often the costs quoted are horrifying and cheaper ways could be equally effective.

By the same token, there is a clear move towards reducing the use of chemicals to deal with weeds, pests and diseases. In practical terms, this is based mainly on a desire to reduce costs, as it is assumed, though of course not always correctly, that chemicals which make the approved list will not be harmful to wildlife in any lasting way. The FWAGs (Farming and Wildlife Advisory Groups) have had an important influence here in making farmers more conscious of the potential alternative treatments of headlands, and the importance of avoiding any chemical encroachment on hedgerows. It is all part of the new thinking about farm operations, which may begin in the wake of efforts to make the odd uncultivated corners of a farm more available to wildlife. It has also been given further impetus by the growing initiatives of the programme known as LEAF (Linking Environment And Farming.)

Such widening of the farming approach has also already been referred to in what Americans call alternative farming. A recent study (1989) reports that 'a growing number of farmers and agricultural researchers are seeking innovative ways to reduce costs and protect human health and the environment'. It goes on to explain the background to this approach.

> Alternative farming practices are not a well-defined set of practices or management techniques, but well-managed alternative farming systems nearly always use less synthetic chemical pesticides, fertilisers and antibiotics than comparable conventional farms. Reduced use of these inputs lowers production costs, and lessens agriculture's potential for adverse environmental and health effects without necessarily decreasing – and in some cases increasing – per acre crop yields and the productivity of livestock management systems... While much work remains to be done, the committee believes that farmers, researchers and policy makers will perceive the benefits of the alternative systems described in this report and will work to make them tomorrow's conventions.

That, in a nutshell, is how farmers both in the USA and Europe are already beginning to adapt their practice to the new horizons of science. But it does not, of course, directly address the global issues of greenhouse gases and possible damage to the ozone layer. However, in Nature's timescale, the purpose behind policies may be more important than the equation they are attempting to balance. It is certainly necessary to think in terms of curbing an imbalance in the carbon cycle but it is questionable whether attempts at a global balance sheet are the best way of deciding how much change is needed. In any scenario, renewable energy is clearly desirable, and its development depends largely on the amount of research put into it, plus some official backing to help it become 'economic'. Likewise, the performance of car engines can clearly be improved beyond recognition once it becomes a major target, and this seems more rational than denouncing the car as an evil in itself. It certainly seems a little strange to be worrying about the methane generated by cows, and still more so to be attempting to compute its global impact. The natural cycle is still vastly more complex than anything man has yet managed to process through his computers. Its adjustment may not so much await his hand on the helm as the abandonment of practices which are detrimental, and a fresh motivation in human society.

When it comes to a balanced environment, European foresters have a much better record than is popularly supposed. An EU report in 1995 noted that the greatest threats were fire and pollution. Pollution is still affecting 25% of the trees in European forests, and that figure is not yet diminishing, though conditions are worse in Central and Eastern Europe than in the West. Nevertheless, since the beginning of the century, the area of forest has been expanding in most countries. Net annual incremental growth is greater than fellings in the whole of the European Union: only in Greece are fellings greater than growth. With the accession of Finland and Sweden, the EU no longer has a negative balance in forestry products, though some two thirds of forest is coniferous and one third deciduous. This, more than anything, reflects the settled nature of European land use, since the conversion of fresh land to agriculture lies well in the past. But it is not necessarily the picture carried by the general public, who tend to believe that obtaining paper from renewable sources is a concept of modern times.

Looking ahead, it is not so difficult to list the things that need to be put right, but it is quite difficult to envisage a fundamental transformation of society. Green policies are certainly contributing to the former, but have yet to make any real impression on the latter. Campaigns are sometimes needed to change a particular situation, but the occupational hazard for campaigners is to become absorbed in achieving their objectives to the exclusion of a wider perspective.

They come to worship the rightness of their cause rather than reaching out to the legitimate concerns of others. The danger, then, is that they seem to represent a kind of alternative society, rather than becoming the leaven in the lump which produces change from within. In the most extreme cases, conventional farming is represented as the source of all evil, when in actual fact it is probably more open to change than it ever has been. The bigger question is what changes are economically viable, and how one can establish a lively rural society, something which many would like to see, but some have written off as unattainable. Organic farming will play its part, but even the most optimistic estimates do not put it as a major component of the farming scene.

Suffice it to say that there will be many paths leading towards change in society, and those which have most to contribute are likely to be those with the deepest spiritual roots. I was quite surprised a few years back to come across the ultimate in urban man at a conference in Switzerland. He expressed no interest at all in poking his nose outside the Conference Hall, and savouring the blessed air of the Swiss mountains. He said: 'I have never been one for the open air life. I do very well indoors and I'm not going to begin looking for fresh air now!' Fortunately, he is the exception which proves the rule, and the great mass of humanity remains committed to renewing its links with the countryside.

Looking at the extent to which the rural balance has been destroyed by commercial development, Jacks and Whyte make an interesting assessment. This was written over fifty years ago.

> If we consider the principal measures which will have to become basic practices in land utilisation, if erosion is to be checked and the soil is to recuperate, it will be obvious that they are quite incompatible with a free competitive economy… The economic efficiency of large scale monoculture and plantation agriculture which form the basis of international trade in food must be superseded by mixed farming, rotational agriculture,

'conservation cropping' and such like practices which cost more in money, labour and thought than monocultural systems.

They were, like Sir George Stapledon, already aware that farming was beginning to go off the rails. 'It must be admitted that applied science has been the prime cause of the dangerous state of exhaustion in which many new countries find themselves today. Science made the free interchange of goods possible throughout the world; it also found less laborious and more efficient ways of producing bread than by the sweat of the brow. Cultivation of the soil became a means to wealth instead of a mode of life. Europe offered an insatiable market for all that the soil could be made to produce, and science increased the soil's production at the expense of its fertility.' While saluting the prescience of their judgement, mankind has not, of course, been totally blind to what was happening. But it has to be admitted that while much has been done to slow down or halt erosion, there has been no fundamental change in economic motivation. Once more the question must be posed, whether more ethical standards will suffice or whether some more fundamental change of attitude is needed to assure the preservation of our soil capital.

That, of course, is the same question raised by the possibility of mankind's behaviour inducing major climatic changes. Whatever the exact degree of danger, that possibility should be enough to make us question seriously the course on which we are navigating at present. But what we may need to understand better is how the democratic process can produce the changes in society which seem to be needed. One scientist of the 1930s predicted that the next great discoveries of mankind would be in the realm of the spirit. At first sight, history would not appear to have justified his prediction, but we may be learning that faith in the Creator could be essential to deepening our understanding of his creation.

One of those who have based their professional life on this foundation is Sir Ghillean Prance, now Director of the Royal

Botanic Gardens at Kew. He has identified a great many economically useful plants which were previously unknown, and is proud that Kew has always respected the proprietary rights of their country of origin. So Kew's network of contacts has enabled his concern for conservation to extend worldwide.

More significantly perhaps, Prance's earlier career was spent largely in the Amazonian rainforest through his association with the New York Botanical Gardens. By 1973 he had been appointed Director of Postgraduate Studies at the National Amazonian Research Institute in Manaus, and it is the continuing work of his Brazilian students which is bringing conservation into the priorities there. Thanks to their influence on the Government, as well as that of others, the destruction of the rainforest has slowed significantly. 'They have done as much for conservation in Brazil as foreigners ever have,' says Prance. 'You can't force a country to care for its environment. You must work from the inside and help it want to do so.'

That must certainly be a lesson for our times, and for the deeper implications it carries for our motivation. The days when Science and Religion could be posed as contradictory guides have largely passed. The not-so-brave new worlds conjured up by Aldous Huxley and George Orwell have made their mark. Their predictions, if not realised to the letter, have been reflected in modern history. For the more we learn about how to do things, the greater is the need for a new motivation to make our discoveries of service to mankind. Even most of those who have no faith would agree that this has somehow to be conjured out of the human spirit. It requires heart and soul as well as brains.

Chapter 6
Animal Welfare and Country Tradition

The environment is the widest of fields, and it has long been under the microscope in many areas. If a new spirit is needed to strike a fresh balance, this is even more true of animal welfare. For animal welfare has until recently been more a question of husbandry than of either morality or science. To start at the beginning of the story is probably to focus on man the hunter and the earliest instincts for survival in the natural world. In such a situation, it was man's welfare that was paramount, and he was no more than one factor in the natural cycle. Hundreds of years of settled farming and the domestication of animals established standards which are still understood and respected today. Questions have been raised, mainly by the advent of so-called factory farming and the development of effective methods for keeping animals in large numbers.

The growth of factory farming has tended to obscure our memories of the traditions of animal husbandry, which are nevertheless alive and well. Increasing knowledge has altered our perceptions, but the commitment of the farmer to his animals has always gone beyond purely financial considerations. A G Street describes most amusingly how the shepherd on his father's farm expected the whole farm to revolve around the needs of his flock, and he was not an isolated phenomenon. The amusement lay in the fact that the portrait was instantly recognisable. Back in the days when I could afford a stockman, Neal was easily able to recall the individual history of several hundred ewes. He would comment on which had had a difficult lambing last year, or how many lambs another had had in the previous three years. For my part, I had to turn to the ear-tags and the written records to make such assessments. This is no bad thing, since it eliminates the errors of a faulty memory, but it marks the entry into a different dimension of livestock husbandry.

So part of the change that has come has been in the numbers involved, and part in our perception of what domestication should involve. In the extremes of factory farming, the accountant has called the tune and, until the whole edifice started to be questioned, his criteria were taken as the only measure of efficiency. These shaped the type of housing used, the push towards a controlled environment, and in the end the escalation of capital costs through over-sophistication. The swing back to outdoor pig keeping is one reaction to this, prompted not so much by a 'back to nature' philosophy as the realisation that in suitable situations first class results can be obtained with much lower capital investment. But it would be a mistake to suppose that all recent experience has been wasted on a blind alley. There have been real achievements, both in breeding and in understanding the physiological performance of stock.

The Farm Animal Welfare Council has called for the phasing out of sow stalls, and intensive study is being made of alternatives to battery cages for hens. There seems little doubt that the Council has achieved a consensus which, if not universally accepted, has the acquiescence of the greater part of the pig and poultry industry. The question of whether we shall be at a disadvantage in the UK if we lead the way in these matters seems to be mainly a question of the speed with which we advance. Given time, I am sure that alternative methods will prove every bit as successful, and there is no point in insisting on a sudden cut-off, when recent investments may not have been written off. Some of those who are not egg producers will have had the experience of visiting battery units where the inmates appear happy enough and the level of conversation indicates contented relaxation rather than unease or boredom. That may often be a valid judgement, since the observer is independent and not involved in this type of production. But those who impute human feelings to animals are on dangerous ground, and would do well to pay more respect to judgements based on daily observation over many years by those who enjoy working with animals. There is certainly no reason to suppose that a hen finds life in a cage more difficult than a budgerigar. Obviously she needs more room than had become usual, but she is a far less athletic figure than the small cage bird, which is accustomed to free flight. This is not to defend the battery system against its critics, so much as to point out that it is far from being the ultimate cruelty sometimes portrayed. All the same, free range eggs are today a growing sector of the egg trade, and a section of the public is prepared to pay a price which leaves a satisfactory profit.

Similarly, with pigs, one has had to study the amount of time used in eating and sleeping, and the natural tendency of the pig to keep its bed clean and to dung elsewhere. Slatted floors have proved their worth where straw is limited, and could perhaps also be more often applied to cattle where feeding areas are involved. It can certainly be affirmed that pig comfort has been a major factor in overall building design. Outside, the pig obviously retains its rooting instinct, and it has been a traditional practice to put rings in the nose where it is necessary to prevent paddocks being turned into a quagmire. Whether the practice would be unacceptable today has hardly been tested, because it does not seem to have been the subject of publicity. However, where a good meal does not have to be sought for, sometimes over considerable distances, the natural inclination of a pig with a full belly is to lie down and have a doze. The revival of keeping wild boar as a diversification well illustrates the variety which domestication has developed!

It is clearly a good thing that the public should take an interest in these issues but, if strong opinions are to be voiced, they need to be based on some investigation of the facts. So often, nothing does more to undermine our trust in daily journalism than to read articles on a subject in which we have some in-depth experience and knowledge. But a raising of journalistic standards can contribute enormously to the value of debate and controversy.

Leaving aside the question of intensive housing, there are many issues of livestock management and medication which are sometimes posed as welfare issues. Extensively produced livestock are generally assumed to be healthier when, in fact, deaths under stress may simply go unrecorded. A friend in Australia, responding to a comment on the carcases of dead sheep around a water hole, remarked that at one time they would have shot those *in extremis*, but now could not afford even to do that. Extreme economic pressure for survival had made it impossible for them to farm as they felt they should. It could equally well be termed an issue of human as of animal welfare. Dry range conditions can be tough, and if animals had the emotions sometimes attributed to them they would envy their cossetted counterparts in more plush conditions. But of course they haven't, and we might well be left reflecting that it is the farmer's way of life which is most in need of rescue.

It is also an indisputable fact that despite the growing lobby for 'natural' meat, it is the chicken industry which has increased its sales in the most spectacular fashion. Despite cracks about the 'rubber chicken' circuit followed by dutiful politicians, such chicken can often be made acceptable by culinary enterprise. Whether anything can be proved against it in terms of the content or quality of the meat is still an open question, but the farmer accepts the principle that the customer is always right. If this sort of chicken is wanted then he must produce it in the volume that is required. So it is at this point that animal welfare or the lack of it must be marked up to public demand. Hopefully, those who are interested will find opportunities increasingly available to meet producers and discuss the points at stake. That problems have arisen in bone structure from such an intensive approach is an established fact, which the industry is trying to address. The assumption by some critics that such problems are simply ignored flies in the face of common sense. All the same, I was interested to discover that a friend in the west of France is producing broilers with an outside run. Possibly they should not be classified as broilers because they are not finished as quickly. But, although he only produces 12,000 at a time, the discerning French public is ready to pay a price which makes this practice a useful pillar in the farm economy.

A growing tendency in recent years has been to use male animals for meat without castration. This has been made possible by earlier maturity and speed of growth. From the point of view of marketing, it remains a controversial area, but in addition to the animal welfare argument, it certainly relieves farmers of a tiresome chore. There seems to be little doubt that it will become established practice for bulls and boars where an economic weight can be achieved at a sufficiently young age. But with ram lambs, there are often complications after weaning, and in many situations it is not possible to guarantee that the great majority will be finished soon enough. It is quite possible to finish them later without having them rejected at the abattoir, but often they may have long periods without making satisfactory progress. This can be true of any lambs, but it does seem to be more common with ram lambs than with wethers, presumably because of their readiness to try to mate with anything, male or female. Castration by rubber rings is extremely convenient, though condemned by a few as unacceptable. The rule that it should be done in the first week of life seems reasonable, and creates no problems. Although some individuals show temporary discomfort (while others none at all) it clearly takes time for the cutting off of the blood supply to have full effect. All the same, subsequent infections are extremely rare, and in my own personal experience virtually unknown.

Wider issues of animal welfare and the impact of science are raised by the use of various growth promoters, often hormones. Here the judgement may be less clear-cut than in the case of housing conditions, and the incentive to use promoters greater when seeking to combat the slower growth of castrates. One of the first discoveries in this field was the predilection of pigs for copper, and the benefits to be gained by including minute amounts of copper in their diet. Such knowledge arose from observing the pig's taste for copper piping, and no-one has questioned the value or propriety of adding copper to their rations. But there is clearly a distinction between trace elements and hormonal growth promoters.

The case of growth hormones for beef steers has already been noted. Perhaps there may be an intrinsic difference of approach as to whether the right question to ask is, do they have harmful effects? Or, do they positively enhance health and performance under the best conditions? This is illustrated in the case of BST (Bovine Somatotropin) where the issue is not the need to achieve higher milk yields but to try and lower the cost of milk production by what can fairly be described as a quick fix. Trials in Canada show that survival rates of cows to the third lactation appear to be substantially lower where BST has been injected, indicating that the stress involved is causing cows to break down before they reach their most productive years. But other trials have given better results, and it is hard for the layman to know where to draw the line.

Much is made of the fact that BST is a naturally occurring hormone, but very little is heard of hormone balance, perhaps because it has not been adequately studied. But it can sensibly be argued that adding an extra quantity of hormone, however natural its occurrence, will have physiological consequences for the cow, as if not the consumer too. As a Canadian dairy farmer points out, if we are content to interfere with an animal's physiological system for a 15% boost in milk production, we may run the risk of masking true genetic merit in our breeding programmes. This could happen if an artificial stimulus allows a cow lacking in natural BST to outshine an animal with a far greater potential for life-time production. High-yielding cows are known to produce more BST than low yielders, so it is reasonable to suppose that if they also show longevity they are well balanced and able to make an invaluable contribution to herd improvement. Even so, the farmer, sitting at his computer, is well aware that he cannot simply confine himself to the figures without making a serious visual assessment of the animals involved.

This also raises a question-mark over the growing popularity of Belgian Blue cattle, which have been bred for their double muscling properties. Their crosses have been winning hands down with the butchers, and the special features of their back ends can easily be seen by the untutored eye! Yet it seems to be accepted that most calves born in purebred herds will be delivered by caesarean section. To most breeders this will be anathema, to be justified if it can be, only by proven economic gains. But having achieved the double-muscling property, is it possible to improve the ease of calving? If I understand aright, Charolais breeders long ago set their faces against breeding for 'double-muscling' precisely because it was likely to exacerbate calving difficulties, even though they were well aware of the extra value attached to the 'culards'. Perhaps this remains a conundrum, for there are now pure Belgian Blue breeders who claim completely natural calving. This is an answer, perhaps, to the Swedes, who proposed banning their breeding in Sweden, but were told this would be illegal inside the EU. Somewhat irrelevantly, I sometimes wonder whether the Belgian Blue is really pleasing aesthetically or whether judgement is swayed only by the knowledge of the extra steak that it will provide! For the present, at any rate, the success of the crosses will continue the breed's growing popularity for use in dairy herds until either other criteria prevail or the calving problems are solved.

Finally, one must touch on transport, where the nature of journeys across the channel has been highlighted by the RSPCA, and where the enforcement of current codes of practice may yet become a serious discouragement to the live trade. For my own part, I have believed all my farming life that it made sense to send stock direct to the abattoir rather than via a market. Logic has largely prevailed in the case of pigs but it has to be said that in the case of cattle and sheep little has changed in the course of a lifetime. There is not much point in arguing about this but, gradually, particularly with the freeing of market forces, the advantages of carcase information and quality payments will become more manifest. Hopefully, too, there will be an improvement in relations between farmers and the abattoirs and meat handlers, whether the ultimate outlet is a conventional butcher or a supermarket. The more care that is given to live transport, the greater will tend to be the economic advantage of transporting carcases. The temptation to cut corners is essentially a temptation to economise. Arguments that, without the live trade, there would be no trade are essentially short-term. The live trade is already a minority interest, and good practice will see it continuing to diminish.

I would not, however, attempt to argue against live transport when it is done with care, as in the export of breeding stock or the movement of race horses. I have a graphic picture in my mind of my friend Tim Harris, a noted livestock exporter, doing battle for his pigs at Lagos airport. It was a moment of acute water shortage, and Tim had been driven to acquire a stock of mineral water in bottles. He had to fight his way back to his charges, almost literally, such was the demand from thirsty humans! Current research is already showing that a long journey is not so much the problem, where stock can lie down and rest. It is even an advantage if they can be fed and watered on board, as it is the loading and unloading which produces stress.

But although one may look forward to a big reduction in the unnecessary transporting of live animals, it is difficult to see the blockading of the ports as serving any useful purpose, still less airports, where travel is likely to be quicker and even better organised. There is no point in interfering with the livelihoods of others when the trade is perfectly legal. Better to recognise that standards can be raised more rapidly through the Farm Animal Welfare Council than through the shouting of slogans. No mention seems to be made of the fact that the Dutch expect all their veal calves to be reared in free housing within another eight years. Changes are under way even across the Channel, but many people seem to have moved their position from wanting proper standards enforced to simply wanting to block even legitimate transport. This is not the place to review the arguments for vegetarianism or to ask what would happen to the world's natural grasslands if such arguments prevailed. But it does suggest that good animal husbandry is still a relevant subject in a scientific age. We may rely less on instinct and traditional country lore, but we are still just as much in need of common sense.

A farming philosophy is needed which shapes our attitude to all value judgements, whether about excellence in production or in transport, slaughtering and marketing. Science and technology can help us achieve things more swiftly and painlessly. There are signs that the demise of the small local slaughterhouse may be succeeded by the advent of the mobile prototype. At least it is a recognition that animals as well as humans may be placed under stress by excessively large-scale operations. Technology can provide the means, but it is still up to the farmer to determine the ends which must be fulfilled. He is the guardian of animal welfare, and must set his heart on targeting improvements rather than giving ground to the unacceptable under the pressure of economics. But, faced with the extremists on animal rights, 'Compassion in World Farming' may have to embrace people as well as animals. It is certainly way over the top to shout insults at lorry drivers and hold up placards suggesting that animals are being consigned to a living hell.

I would be a lot happier, too, if the RSPCA confined itself to issues of cruelty, and did not set itself up to appraise standards of meat production, in which it is not strictly competent. Organic and Farm Assured initiatives are well under way, and would be better reinforced than faced with yet another category. Feelings give rise to a perfectly valid expression of concern, but are not an adequate basis on which to erect a balanced judgement. As one leading scientist involved in these matters wrote to me, 'A subject like animal welfare is enormous, and a systematic examination requires a whole (large) book, and indeed they exist. Even a comparative assessment of one's own experience against the views expressed in such books would be a big job.'

For this reason, I have confined my observations to a single chapter, and accept that it must be selective and incomplete. It is probably true, moreover, that even the largest tome on the subject would not leave one with an undisputed blueprint for change. So far as the European Union is concerned, there are also national and cultural differences to be overcome, and self-righteousness is the great enemy of open discussion in such a forum. There is much readiness to make progress, but it cannot be fulfilled by just laying down the law, as some campaigners tend to do. This is a discussion to which farmers have much to contribute from the background of a long tradition in animal care. Those who sometimes cite statistics of lamb losses at or soon after birth as evidence of lack of care show a woeful ignorance of the facts. All who spend long hours in shepherding are committed at lambing time to a degree of care that is always sacrificial of personal convenience. It owes nothing to any calculation of economic gain against time involved. At its most basic, that is in many ways the heart of the matter. Good training may make shepherds' efforts more effective, but it will fulfil rather than replace their motivation.

Chapter 7
Farming Satisfactions –
What Makes a Way of Life?

If animal welfare is not easy to define in a comprehensive fashion, the essence of the farming way of life may prove even more elusive. There are some things in life that defy analysis. But there is an extensive literature of the countryside in English which proves our preoccupation with country pleasures and country values. For some, this represents a romanticised view of a past which never existed. For others, it is a reality that is now long gone. Yet for all who work on the land there are memories which linger as realities that have been lived and enjoyed. Some of the things one feels about a calling in life are highly individual, others are perceptions shared by rural society as a whole.

The natural world teaches us a great deal, and much of it we take for granted. It may well be that in some highly populated countries which lack open spaces, a true communion with wild life is almost ended. It could be so in Britain, though happily there are signs that we are drawing back from its extinction. The wilderness must be able to impose itself to make its point with man. It has to remain beyond our understanding and a stimulus to the imagination.

The dictionary defines imagination as a creative faculty of the mind, but it is not simply a faculty that one can call up and control, though it can certainly be cultivated. It is also stimulated by experience, and is often most evident in childhood because it is to a great extent spontaneous. It is something that we cannot consciously create but only learn to harness, hence the phrase 'imagination that runs riot', because it is a faculty that pours forth without making moral judgements, though it may well reflect the furniture of our mind. At my childhood home, there was a shrubbery beyond the formal garden which was actually called 'the wilderness'. Objectively speaking, it did not entirely merit that description, but it proved a potent stimulus to the imagination in a way which the formal garden did not.

In imagination, however, we are all to some extent the children of our times, and in some degree formed by them. My early thoughts of becoming a gamekeeper owed much to expeditions with a gun, either alone or with my brother, through fields and woods around our home. But it also owed something to the literature which explored the skill of the hunter and celebrated his tenacity and triumphs. Sometimes in recording those skills, it also recoiled at the way modern technology threatens to snuff them out.

A writer like Richard Jefferies charmed not only with his descriptions of nature, but with the challenge of pulling off a good shot in the days when it was necessary to light a match or strike a flint. Indeed, to some extent he deplored the perfection of more modern guns, whose efficiency made success so much easier. 'To wander out into the brake, to creep from tree to tree so noiselessly that the woodpecker should not cease to tap – in that there is joy. The consciousness that everything depends on your personal skill, and that you have no second resource if that fails you, gives the real zest to sport.'

Jefferies also remarks that destruction in itself is not the motive, rather an overpowering instinct for woods and fields. He scorns the idea of taking part in highly organised shoots where large bags are recorded, and I have felt something of the same reaction in driving across country in a Land Rover, where formerly I had walked. Technology in that sense can become an insulation from reality. I would not quarrel with those who like to put down large numbers of hand-reared pheasants, but I do not think that such occasions could ever fully satisfy my spirit, because for me the pleasure of the occasion does not lie in the number of cartridges fired or birds killed.

By the same token, Peter Scott, crouching with a gun in the half light, first knew the thrill of wild geese flighting on the marshes . He came to prefer commemorating them in his paintings, and finished by creating the wildfowl sanctuary at Slimbridge. For some people, this would seem to imply a sudden conversion, but it may in reality have been much more a natural progression. Certainly, many who might have gone to shoot big game for trophies in Africa, have been diverted into the arts of photography and filming, which are the road to a much more comprehensive understanding of the animals involved.

That unlikely hero of the hunting field, the Cockney tea merchant John Jorrocks created by R S Surtees, declared, 'It ar'n't that I loves the fox less, but that I loves the 'ound more.' But he inevitably blotted his copy book with the anti-hunting fraternity, when he called hunting the sport of kings. 'The image of war without its guilt and only five and twenty percent of its danger.' A far cry perhaps from Masefield's Robin Dawe, a more recent huntsman.

> So, in Dawe's face, what met the eye
> Was only part; what lay behind
> Was English character and mind,
> Great kindness, delicate sweet feeling
> (Most shy, most clever in concealing
> Its depth) for beauty of all sorts,
> Great manliness and love of sports,
> A grave, wise thoughtfulness and truth,
> A merry fun outlasting youth,
> A courage terrible to see
> And mercy for his enemy.
>
> (from 'Reynard the Fox')

This diversion into country sports is not entirely irrelevant, as the preoccupation of its literature with character goes to show. This preoccupation has endured through the centuries, and it may be worth more than a passing thought about the watershed at which it seems to have arrived today. Even children can distinguish between realistic and purely romantic stories of wild life. They can appreciate the reality of stories such as *Tarka the Otter* or *Bannertail the Squirrel*, while equally enjoying the fantasy of *The Wind in the Willows*. In many cases they may be more down-to-earth than those grown-ups whose imagination persists in endowing animals with human personality and feelings. On a different level, of course, *Animal Farm* or *Watership Down* use animals to symbolise the human condition, and it is a symbolism which works. But it is aimed at saying more about the human than the animal world, albeit that there is a certain connecting thread.

Some people find it hard to sit and observe nature run its course. There is a compulsion to interfere and check apparent cruelty and the prodigal waste of life, even though life is being continuously created in abundance. For me, one of the charms of David Attenborough's programmes on television, is the way he is content to observe and expound without a hint of moralising. We have to ponder the ways of an established order in which we have had no part except to be present. Even in our well-founded urge to save the planet from possible disaster, the key is not so much in preserving the ozone layer or reducing greenhouse gases, as in understanding its Creator. His ways are not our ways, and it will be His ways which carry the day. That perhaps is why some imaginative works seem to have a timeless quality which gives them life through many centuries. In this age of tourism we tend to laugh a little at the Shakespeare industry, but one can only marvel at the effect of his plays on all English-speaking people, not only those for whom English is their native language. Go back far enough, of course, and everything has links with the farming tradition. Farming as a way of life was a central part of national life. It is only more recently that it has become side-lined, and its future called in question, as rural society has come to embrace many other elements.

But such values do not become quickly dated. Leo Tolstoy, most widely known probably for his novel *War and Peace*, was a Russian landowner who became intensely preoccupied with our way of life a hundred years ago. He espoused so many ideas and convictions in the course of a long life that A N Wilson, one of his biographers, detects a wilful absence of common sense in his efforts to live out his Christianity. But Wilson is on more dubious ground when he suggests that Tolstoy's religion is 'ultimately the most searching criticism of Christianity there is. He shows that it does not work.'

Wilson also records that Lenin, watching Tolstoy from abroad, was fascinated by the glaring contradictions in Tolstoy's works, ideas and teaching. He was chiefly struck by the contradiction between the incomparable artist and what he called 'the landowner obsessed by Christ'. He felt it was symptomatic of 'those contradictory conditions in which the historical activity of the peasantry in our Revolution was set...' Lenin saw that the interests of different groups of people must ultimately find a political expression. Wilson comments, 'This is common sense and therefore Tolstoy rejected it. But with the wise and imaginative part of himself, he saw that if you refuse to soil your hands with power, there will be others who are not so squeamish.' But it was from Tolstoy that Mahatma Gandhi developed the idea of passive resistance, and then proceeded to prove it in practice.

Moreover, Tolstoy's description in *Anna Karenin* of Levin's (a character supposedly modelled on himself) desire to join his serfs mowing in the hay field with scythes, evokes a universal recognition of so many such encounters across the class divide. It features all the feelings of the boss trying to prove himself both in stamina and skill through a hard day's work. Then it describes the ultimate acceptance of his men, some critical and some sympathetic, who extend their fellowship, while the bolder spirits do not shrink from teasing or criticising. It is a scene that could be paralleled in England even in the 1920s or early 1930s. Tolstoy also makes the further point that manual labour can bring a satisfaction and fulfilment which, contrary to popular supposition, actually stimulates creative thought.

At a time when Russia is struggling to come to terms with a private enterprise economy, and combat the grip of the Mafia money-makers, it is interesting that those who want to understand

Russia are often recommended to read Tolstoy and Dostoyevsky. It is not just advocacy of an academic exercise, but part of the understanding of a way of life, which, although changing through the years, owes its mainspring to the sources of national character and motivation which are deep in its culture. Certainly neither writer shrinks from an examination of the depths of evil and the need for repentance. Both in their different ways assert a belief in Russia's destiny, while expounding the plentiful contradictions to be found in human nature.

There are undoubtedly things in farming which help in ironing out some of these contradictions. One thing that is unique to farming is the fact that the farm is both workplace and home. This has enormous advantages for family life. The farmer has only to walk out of the house to be at work, and he can easily spend time with the children in place of his wife while she attends to her own jobs whether on the farm or further afield. Then, as the children grow up, they can participate in the farm's activities. A Swedish friend remarked the other day that he had nine children, and they all helped on the farm!

This can have certain complications in our mechanised age, and there are also dangers to guard against, as occasional accidents remind us, but it does seem that the farmer's way of life can survive, and that it may yet be as valued in the future as it has been in the past. There is a deep and universal pleasure in seeing a farm reclaimed from neglect or raised to a new level of fertility. The well known quote from Jonathan Swift's *Gulliver's Travels*, can bear repeating. 'And he gave it for his opinion, that whoever could make two ears of corn or two blades of grass to grow upon a spot of ground where only one grew before, would deserve better of mankind and do more essential service to his country than the whole race of politicians put together.'

Some of these satisfactions come by the sweat of the brow, and some more as a gift of God. So there is perhaps a temptation to put oneself more in the way of the latter! I was never a great enthusiast for hoeing and singling sugar beet. It tended to produce backache, but it was a wonderful sight to see the change wrought on a weedy field, while a few weeks later it would seem like a minor miracle. There was something of a turning point when the small strip hoed in a large field widened to become the greater half, and there was a growing hope of fulfilment.

In a different context, the improvement of a permanent pasture which has been under-grazed over many years can also bear witness to the pleasure of getting things right. Extra stock put pressure on the less productive species, and with time and good management the balance of good grasses and white clover improves. To the farmer, this is a matter of deep satisfaction quite apart from the extra output that he may be able to achieve. He has in his mind's eye a picture of the perfect pasture, and this has nothing at all in common with the popular nostalgia for meadows full of wild flowers. Yet he is the rightful heir of the man who created those meadows, and the creator of a new tradition which still keeps faith with an ideal of good farming. If meadows full of wild flowers are wanted, they can be created, but we must not fail to realise that modern grassland management is practising lessons learned through the years, and effectively building up soil fertility to new levels. Farming is about how men cultivate or work with the land. Wilderness is about leaving things to nature. There may be bridges between the two, but we must always clearly define our aims. Otherwise farmers will be wrongly criticised for doing their job in food production, and public perceptions will fail to come to grips with the facts of the matter.

Meanwhile it is undeniable that advancing mechanisation has taken a lot of the sweat out of farming, and that brain rather than brawn may now be predominant. Gone are the days when physical prowess and sheer stamina could command respect. They have been replaced by good planning and the professional and painstaking application of available knowledge to the tasks in hand. Some specialisation is inevitable, but there is a call for wider judgements which can weigh up the relative merits of different systems or the way in which all things can work together for the good of the farm as a whole.

This may cut both ways, in the sense that the farmer is more frequently at his desk. But like new toys, the computer soon settles down to being a tool for doing certain jobs, and producing certain information. When I first came home to farm, I remember walking with a farming friend through a pasture with a fine show of buttercups in flower. He remarked, 'You'll need to spray these out,' and in due course I did so to the great improvement of the pasture concerned. But this did not fill me with an automatic desire to use chemicals at the drop of a hat. They were simply another tool added to the armoury, and with the knowledge that there was no way I could have achieved the same elimination of the buttercups without ploughing. It added a new dimension that one did not possess before.

Such new possibilities may lead one a bit further away from dependence on the basics, and in that sense may induce a false sense of power over natural forces. But here I think farmers must learn a lesson from the scientist. In my experience, good scientists are marked by a certain humility, and above all by an awareness of what they don't know and what still needs to be learned. This is the best insurance against the Greeks' *hubris*, which marked one down as meet for destruction by the Gods!

So while it can be asserted that the farmer's way of life is still based on the same values, it is clear that it has to relate to a rather different world and an increasingly materialist society. In this situation, example is better than precept, but one has to speculate on the implication for personal values in our society which are, after all, the lifeblood of democracy. No farmer, for example, who observes homosexuality among farm animals can doubt that it is a natural phenomenon. But observation also suggests that it is against natural laws, for in the great majority of cases it does not persist. Having been at a boys' boarding school, I had always imagined that most of those I knew to be practising homosexuals would grow out of it. In the present climate of opinion, I have sometimes since wondered whether that was the case or not. It may be dangerous to make such an assumption, but I am in no doubt that we get many chances to choose in deciding the road we will follow. Animals follow their instincts, but man has a faculty for decision that goes beyond his instincts.

Such affection as animals show has no connection with sex, though it may be connected with food! But the farmer's care in tending his stock calls mainly for the sacrifice of his own time and comfort in ministering to their needs. It also has to do with health, and sensitivity to signs of illness or discomfort, so that success in feeding and breeding brings a visual reward in the well-being of the stock. But as with all living things, crises have a strange habit of occurring at weekends. When livestock get out, it may be because they have been held in a fraction too long on a particular pasture, though it can also be simply a gate left open. To restore order, patience and flexibility are often called on, and tempers are tested if the trouble is seen to be caused by an earlier failure to grasp the nettle, so often true in the case of weak fencing. My friend John Brodie had a great way of defusing such situations. Ringing up to report that our stock were in his field, his opening gambit would be, 'This is your favourite neighbour...'

But there is a wider sense in which the farming way of life contributes to spiritual values. The farming calendar records the passing seasons, but it also beats in time with eternity. Farming character equates with the farmer's way of life. Right and wrong have always been part of it, and common sense provides no climate for semantic quibbling or hair splitting. When I married Kristin, the early years gave us a good many laughs over our different views of time. Frequently she would ask me to do something, and I would say yes, meaning I would put it on my list of jobs and find a time for it in due season, perhaps next week, next month or even next year! The next day she would ask me in a puzzled way why I hadn't done it. I don't know which of us was most surprised at the yawning gap between our respective views of time; and it has continued to be a source of amusement.

Yet whatever the perspective on time, there is an abiding faith that seed time and harvest will be accomplished in the end, whatever the adverse conditions encountered. There is also a shrewd idea of what is needed to make the most of a situation, and not to let an opportunity slip through the fingers. I well remember, when I was serving my apprenticeship as a farm pupil in Oxfordshire, how our neighbours were always behind with their work. There was a certain fecklessness about their approach which ensured that they were always behind the clock. Sometimes to catch up in the week, they would go plodding on through Sundays. On such an occasion, one of the men on our side of the hedge observed sagely, 'If they can't do it in six days, they won't do it in seven'. Yet he would have been instantly ready to turn out on Sunday if it were a question of saving hay in a catchy time or stooking sheaves to avoid sprouting.

Back in those days, it used to be debated whether farming was a business or a way of life. The usual conclusion was that it had to be a bit of both; but it would perhaps be truer to say that we need to make economics a part of our way of life, and not the dominant theme. In more recent times, the Common Agricultural Policy has led some to believe that a choice has to be made between economic and social objectives, or even that a kind of two-tier development may come into play, with the go-getters out in front and the more environmentally concerned (and by implication less efficient) bringing up the rear.

But if farming life means anything, it has to be seen as a balanced whole. The true professional seeks technical excellence for its own sake more than for the profit that may result. What science is unveiling for us is exciting, and it stirs the blood as the range of possibilities become apparent. At the same time, the growing network of universal and immediate communication makes the knowledge available to all those with access to education.

For the first time, grape growers in California and Maharashtra are studying the same procedures. Potato growers in Scotland and Zimbabwe have common ground on virus diseases. In practical terms, this unity of purpose does not spring from a common culture, but from a common approach to the possibilities of soil and climate in all their diversity. The mistake would be to suppose with Marx that economic considerations are paramount, and will in the long run shape human society. It is an understandable mistake, because it is abundantly clear that the common reality of the situation today is that those with money are the first to benefit from new knowledge. Our pursuit of a way of life that goes beyond this will have to be established, and it may not be fanciful to believe that farmers could help to show the way.

Outside farming, too, the concept of 'a way of life' may be due for fresh recognition as an embodiment of values without a rigid ideological or systematic framework. It represents the establishment of a solid link between what you believe and what you do. Religion, of course, provides the prime examples when seen as a life to be lived rather than as mere adherence to dogma or membership of an institution.

It is concern with a way of life which seems to have motivated Alexander Solzhenitsyn to return to his native land. He came home to Russia to serve his motherland, not to preach but to offer the lessons of hard experience. It is no easy thing for a man in his seventies, after years of dedicated writing in exile, to journey home with his wife, meeting the people, listening and talking to all who may cross his path. Yet even the sometimes indifferent press photographs seemed to show a man who had shed a burden and come home with joy to the country he loves. Those in the West who have been stung by his criticisms of us here miss the point when they feel he does not understand the good things or label reactionary his unswerving commitment to honesty. They may quibble about his qualities as an historian but, more than anyone else, he sees the Russian destiny in historical terms.

Before his return, he spoke of the people on whom he pinned his hopes.

In the numerous letters I have received from the Russian provinces, from the expanses of Russia, I have descried during these years spiritually healthy people dispersed across her breadth, often young, but disunified, lacking spiritual nourishment. Upon returning to my homeland, I hope to see many of them. Our hope is pinned precisely and exclusively on this healthy nucleus of living people. Perhaps as they grow, influence each other, and join efforts, they will gradually revitalise our nation. (*The Russian Question at the End of the 20th Century*, Harvill Press, 1995)

Solzhenitsyn does not set himself up as an authority, and still less does he wish for political power. Yet he seeks the resurrection of the Russian way of life, and people sense that he has the rocklike integrity which has been so much lacking. It could be a way of life for the present which is at one with both the past and the future. That is the secret of a stable society. Can Russian farmers conceivably reclaim this heritage? Such a thought is not often in the minds of Westerners who seek to help them.

It is not only Russia that may be in need of a new way of life. My friend Stanislaw Choma in Poland has always been a supporter of family farming, and has weathered the vicissitudes of recent history better than most. He once described ruefully how he borrowed money from the bank to buy a pig, only to find when it had grown to killing weight that its value would not repay the loan. More serious disappointments have assailed him, but they have not prevented him from being a tower of strength to others in his locality who have had to wrestle with the difficulties of transition.

Rural Solidarity led the battle to defend Poland's family farms from communist collectivisation. As a result, 80% of the land remained in private ownership until the liberation. But the sudden collapse of communism removed the mainspring from the struggle, and raised the spectre of how to live with former communist officials whose hands on the levers of power allowed them to profit from the problems of privatisation. Stanislaw himself had suffered from unprovoked aggression from the police, which landed him in hospital. But, lying in a hospital bed, he had time to reflect, and was freed from the bitterness which could have taken hold and coloured his subsequent attitude. So at a time when the membership of Rural Solidarity has fallen dramatically, Stanislaw's local branch boasts 5000 members.

This can be mainly ascribed to the care and service he has provided, both officially and unofficially. From a strong family base, he has offered contract services with his machinery at a reasonable price, and this has helped him to keep in touch with the needs of local families. One friend who had fallen on hard times turned to drink, and very soon his marriage was breaking up. Stanislaw, who like so many of his countrymen is a devout Catholic, had the thought to visit him and see if he could help. When he knocked on the door, husband and wife were locked in a fierce shouting match and didn't hear him. Standing there, he felt he had come too late and, getting cold feet, was tempted to turn away. But he persisted and crossed the threshold to find himself warmly welcomed by both antagonists.

To cut a long story short, his friend found freedom from alcohol, his marriage was remade and, with a loan from Stanislaw, he was able to get a viable business going. Such care beyond the call of duty is the lifeblood of village communities. In all essentials, it could also be the lifeblood of the European Union, if we focused on such values, and committed ourselves to making it people-friendly. That is the significance of a way of life worth perpetuating.

Chapter 8
Lessons of Experience

One cannot look back on a lifetime in farming without sensing the power of its way of life just described. How many times does one hear the cause of family farming invoked? And how frequently is it followed by the demand for a definition of family farming? Our conceptions may be very much coloured by personal experience, but at the same time they may also have a wider and universal validity.

It is sometimes surprisingly hard to remember just how things seemed when one experienced them, still more the sequence of events which have led to particular conclusions. But there is no doubt about the tenor of the impressions which remain, and which are a part of farming history as surely as the characters and events which feature in the public memory. That is part of the significance with which our individual lives are endowed by God, and which makes democracy a meaningful conception, over and above all its political divisions and confusions. There is a thread in history, even though most individual lives leave no visible mark, and some well-known leaders earn no more than a fleeting mention on the written page. There is a collective perception which reflects the change of outlook from age to age, and even from one decade to another. Perhaps such perceptions are enhanced by universal education and instant communication, and perhaps in that sense life does move faster than it used to. The fact remains that such perceptions do take root, and are real. Equally, they change and are in flux on the road to the next milestone.

For all these reasons, experience, like truth, can be a two-edged sword. We know the truth of what we have lived, but we may fail to draw the right conclusion for those who come after us. One doesn't have to be a Luddite or an arch conservative to hanker for known ways. But the fact remains that however up-to-date a new method of working, it can soon be overtaken by events. Experience can be a great guide or a dangerous dictator. The acid test may be whether we can keep on learning new lessons.

Farming in the 1950s, for me, saw a transition from the old to the new, from mixed farming to expanding acreages and thoughts of a more specialised approach. The last working horse we had went out in a blaze of glory when he bolted with an empty cart, galloped unimpeded through some iron railings and only came to rest when the cart overturned half way across the next field. Thereafter he became unmanageable, and the last expedition to fetch a water cart parked in a pasture was a precarious triumph of mind over matter. Certainly, if he had upped the pressure only slightly I could not have held him. But although thoughts of increasing mechanisation were already dawning, a brief reality of the day was two hundredweight sacks of grain dumped on the fields by the combine as the binder was finally relegated.

Early experiments with self-feed silage were on a minimal scale by modern standards, and were complicated by the length of the material ensiled. Getting it out of the clamp was hard work for both beast and man. How much easier if precision chop harvesters had already been in the field. Quality lucerne hay played its part for a number of years, though it had to be made on tripods stacked by hand, which themselves then had to be finally swept up by buckrake to a stationary baler. Beef cattle were still dominated by the Hereford, and anything without a white face was at a disadvantage in the local store market. Cattle rearing was still traditional, and in our area based on permanent grass, though the concept of ley farming had also made its impact. Its adoption was mainly limited by the frequency of steep slopes.

It was also the time when I bought my first sheep, which were Clun Forest or their crosses and, contrary to the cattle, black faces found favour in the market for store lambs. Shortly afterwards, I went to confer with Oscar Colburn on the question of sheep recording, after he had designed a Record Book printed by *Farmer and Stockbreeder*. I stuck to the recording, but not so long after that,

Oscar started his work on the Colbreds, and I failed to find anyone else among the Clun Forest breeders who felt strongly about the importance of records in a breeding programme. Later, I was to meet Tom Fulton, farm manager for the Institute of Animal Physiology at Babraham, but by that time I had some doubts as to whether the Cluns were the best breed for our purpose.

North Herefordshire may have been less developed than many English counties, as those were also years of the digging of septic tanks, the installation of running water and the connection with an electricity supply. It soon becomes hard to remember the days of Tilly paraffin lamps used for evening reading, and still more so their somewhat risky use to bring warmth to sows and litters at farrowing. I can, however, well remember on one occasion burning the bristles on the back of a large white sow, though she herself showed hardly any visible reaction to the experience! So although science was at work, and knowledge was growing, it was still what might have been described as traditional farming, in which labour-intensive practices were still the norm.

Cultivation by trailed rather than powered implements meant reliance on winter frosts for a good tilth, and a stronger sense of being bound to the weather than obtained later. It was nevertheless a relief to advance from horse-drawn implements fitted with tractor drawbars to equipment actually designed for tractors, and frequently with the luxury of being driven by power take-off. Harry Ferguson, with his little grey tractor and three-point linkage, had pioneered the pattern of the future, and soon our David Brown was coming into line. As the ending of World War II steadily receded into the past, a spirit of expansion and development took hold.

Advancing into the sixties, changes began to accelerate. We had the opportunity to add a second farm (already owned but previously tenanted) thus advancing from 130 acres to 280 acres and establishing a specialised piggery in one set of buildings. Fields were enlarged and some hedges and fences were removed to allow for cultivating areas over 10 acres rather than under. At the same time, with the pressure to add to the cultivated area, two pastures were subdivided to allow areas with a suitable contour to be ploughed. There was certainly a net loss of hedges on the farm but, looking out on the field pattern today, I remain convinced that it is an improvement from every point of view. It has been carried through without any disadvantage to wildlife, and anyone looking at this countryside would be quite unaware of what has been done.

Although the piggery at its inception was aimed only at a herd of forty sows, it included a forerunner of building trends to come, in the first production model of the Peers-Ballard fattening house. The unit was even the subject of a programme on Midlands TV, a vivid reminder of how quickly such early initiatives were overtaken by a veritable flood of new building design. Today it might be said that the wheel has come full circle with a move to outdoor pig-keeping, where this is possible, with a view to lowering capital costs. At the same time, a great many indoor herds are swinging back to natural ventilation, less extreme early weaning and a realisation that simpler buildings can still produce an equal performance. The search for the perfect farrowing set-up has called forth a great deal of ingenuity, but it is doubtful whether it has made farrowing a much more foolproof exercise at the end of the day. The Solari House, which has been in use for a great many years, can probably still produce results that equal the best.

At the same time, it has to be said that all the work put in has greatly enlarged our knowledge of the vast potential in pig production. But advances in breeding and nutrition have sometimes perhaps masked the fact that it was not always the improvements wrought by controlled environment which could claim the credit for more efficient growth and production. I have never been a great supporter of sow stalls, but they were undoubtedly created from a desire to try and give individual treatment to sows in large units. That they have been called in question and scheduled for phasing out may reflect some of the limitations of large units, despite the undoubted successes achieved in them. This is not the place to debate the issue, but arguments based on grounds of efficiency and low cost are far from making an open and shut case. The Meat and Livestock Commission recording figures and the desire to be numbered in the top third on performance have been invaluable in reflecting achievements from year to year. But it is probable that the wish to keep control of breeding operations is a bigger factor than cost of production in the creation of units running into hundreds or even thousands of sows.

Where this has led to excessive concentrations of pigs and consequent pollution problems, experience surely shows it to be a flawed development. Yet it would be a mistake not to salute the example of pioneers such as Ken Woolley and his friends with the Pig Improvement Company. They were among the first to lead the way, even if some traditionalists raised an eyebrow at the launching of a new pig in the plush surroundings of Claridges!

The decade of the seventies saw a further thrust to increase food production with a free, and sometimes unthinking, rein given to technology. The UN World Food Conference held at Rome in 1974 was called to consider urgently the threat of world food shortage and famine. Even such a short time afterwards, it is hard to recall the mood in which such an assembly was convened or the shock to the assumption of cheap energy caused by the formation of OPEC (Organisation of Petroleum Exporting Countries).

In our own farming, it saw the addition of a further 90 acre farm to the enterprise, with the farmhouse being sold off separately. Though mostly hilly, with a valley stream, it extended the possibilities for beef and sheep production and brought a small increase to the cereal acreage. Machinery could more easily be justified, and my thoughts turned to grass-drying as a possible avenue to solve the perennial search of the grassland farmer for high quality feed in winter. I had seen at a nearby farm, before the war, the possibilities of dried grass as a feed for milk production, albeit produced by burning coal with a generous application of manpower. However, it had enabled the farmer, a producer-retailer with a substantial

Ayrshire herd, to produce milk on home-grown feed at a time when the cheapest imports were available from all over the world. In a trial to test dried grass as the sole feed, the loss of yield per cow was no more than fifty gallons in a lactation, for a herd averaging just under 1000 gallons. It had seemed to me the ultimate vindication of grassland farming as a self-contained operation.

Events were subsequently to prove me wrong and, though I did not entirely regret making the attempt, it was easy to see with hindsight how time and effort could have been better spent. Examination of various approaches to hay drying showed that all had some disadvantages in terms of labour or quality control, though these were not necessarily insuperable. My major misjudgement on drying was in weighing up the engineering soundness of the Hayflaker machine. Being no great shakes as a mechanic, my prime concern was to satisfy myself that I could operate the machine without help. I decided that I could, but fatally underestimated the fire risk which arose from sparks thrown off from the burner when the grass was nearly dry. A final warning was granted almost at the point of decision when Kristin overheard an animated exchange of fire stories by other users of the machine. They were in jovial mood, but the point should have been taken! Not only does a serious fire dislocate the work, but it has a psychological effect which weighs on subsequent operations! The actual rise in the oil price was substantial, but had been allowed for and was not fatal, economically speaking. With wilting, we could dry grass sometimes at rates as low as 30-35 gallons per ton. This also helped the throughput, which was another brake on the total viability of the system. But it was a blunder to suppose that burning fossil fuel, however economical it might appear, was a sensible proceeding. The Hayflaker was finally sold to the only operator left, a canny dairy farmer in Ayrshire, whose expertise was such that he not only never had a fire, but used the automatic controls which even the inventor did not entirely trust. I remember the latter confessing to me how his Scottish host invited him for a cup of coffee while the load finished drying, and he was on tenterhooks lest the system came unstuck and a fire resulted.

So ended the grass drying experiment, though the final product was a joy to feed, and a sure way to maintain the health and performance of cattle and sheep. But it would have been wiser to pursue the rapid advances being researched in silage making or the potential of barn dried hay, while accepting that it was impossible to be totally insulated from adverse weather. Certainly, the urge to preserve the incomparable value of grass in the field was a major motivating force, but there are many complexities in making an overall farming judgement. There can be no denying the value of the baler, but the potential for loose handling, even beyond the small farm scale, was perhaps neglected. One of the simplest systems I have seen for handling barn-dried hay was an electric grab on an overhead rail, which could remove a couple of hundredweight at a bite from the loose stack and deposit it wherever the rail might run.

A sabbatical round-the-world journey in 1977/78 convinced me of the need for low-cost farming. It became increasingly clear that regardless of the scale on which one was operating, high-cost operations were bound to be more vulnerable. Obviously, low-cost farming began with looking for ways of eliminating the overdraft and farming without any major obligation to the Bank. But it also entailed looking for appropriate technology rather than simply the ultimate in convenience, labour saving and sophistication. For the first time, questions had to be asked about the possibility of oversophistication and, in the case of livestock farming, the merits of a man's annual wage against the capital cost of increased mechanisation.

Grazed grass remains the trump card to be exploited, and on this farm winter feeding centres on grass silage and home-grown barley. Whole crop silage or even maize may have to be considered in addition. Out-of-season lambing has been discarded in favour of lambing to meet the grass, and stubble turnips play an important part in finishing later lambs. The Lleyn flock has become the main source of prolific ewe replacements, and these are crossed with the graded-up Texel flock, which also produces the terminal sires. The emergence of the Lleyn from rare breed status to challenge for the prolificacy and type needed today has been a great encouragement. The breeding group, which has survived some difficult vicissitudes, is now providing useful comparisons and measurable progress.

It is a largely self-contained system, and the cattle have moved in the same direction. Where previously young cattle were bought in for finishing, mainly at the suckler sales, a suckler herd has now been established to produce the cattle at home. Hereford x Friesian heifers were used to start the herd, and a Simmental bull is being used with a view to keeping homebred heifers for replacement. As might be expected, the main opportunities for improvement lie in grassland management, animal breeding and the overall integration of the system.

For us, grassland management has moved away from Italian and hybrid ryegrasses towards longer-term perennials and white clover, giving leys of at least four years duration. It remains to be seen whether talk of extensification can lead to a longer grazing season or other economies. For the moment, stocking rate remains an important factor financially, and one of the keys to profit on any given area.

On questions of mechanisation, the escalation in the price of larger machines has led to an increase in the work being done by contractors, both for silage-making and harvesting. At the same time, the advent of ATVs (All Terrain Vehicles) has opened up fresh possibilities. Begun as an approach to low ground pressure work when land is too wet to take the weight of conventional tractors, the ATVs have shown a further ability to cut costs. In fertiliser spreading and crop spraying they have shown themselves cheaper to operate than tractors; while for going round livestock they are unmatched, not only for cost but for getting round fields to every hidden corner without leaving a mark. They are undoubtedly a cost-effective answer in many circumstances.

In crop production, as already noted, a fair amount of scientific research is being directed to the possibility of a reduction of inputs being achieved without a commensurate drop in output. 'Integrated Production', as it seems to be called in Europe, is fast becoming a major trend. In Switzerland, under the influence of official Government policy, 30% of the farmers are reckoned to be following a clearly-defined integrated programme. This is part of a government strategy for the whole industry, in which steps are laid out right up to 2002. A timely example of government forethought which we might well covet for Brussels.

The Americans suggest that the hallmark of an alternative farming approach is not the conventional practices it rejects but the innovative practices it includes. 'The objective is to sustain and enhance, rather than reduce and simplify the biological interactions on which production agriculture depends, thereby reducing the harmful off-farm effects of production practices. Many of today's common practices were the alternative practices of the post-war era. One example is monocultural production, which synthetic fertilisers and pesticides made possible. The widespread adoption of these alternatives, referred to internationally as the Green Revolution, led to dramatic increases in yield per acre and overall production in the US and many other countries.' That crop rotation may now be seen to be desirable does not detract from the achievements of the last 25 years. Big increases in Indian wheat and rice production have been sustained without an increase in the cultivated area.

These are all straws in the wind, and the wind would seem to be blowing steadily, regardless of whether the CAP finds a fresh lease of life or we end up in a New Zealand subsidy-free scenario. There is an increasing range of things that can be done, but that is not to say that they are necessarily worth doing. More choices have to be made, and it may even pay not to be in too big a hurry. More time may need to be spent on forward strategies and less on the competitive urge to gain a tactical advantage.

If you are not doing a job yourself, experience shows that it is the man you employ who usually determines the success of the operation, whether it is getting the job done to time or getting it done well. In pig production, I have found that the ups and downs of the pig cycle are easily dwarfed by the ups and downs caused by a change of pigman! These are no doubt lessened by better education and professional training, but they remain at the root of motivation and debate about man management.

Our tractor driver has now been with us many years, and he cares for the farm and approaches it as if it were his own. Yet the confidence between us has not been lightly won. Even after a number of years together, he once got angry and gave me notice because I had asked him to let a student, who was with us, continue ploughing a field he had started, in order to get experience. Next day he withdrew his notice, and I discovered the insecurity he felt about his job. He had thought I might be tempted to get more work done on contract, and use student labour to fill in, thus making him redundant. Nothing could have been further from my mind, but it was an important lesson in communication.

Experience is a continuing road, and there is no ultimate point of arrival. It remains what is termed a learning process, and one in which all can share! I am often amazed to hear people say that if they had their time again, they wouldn't do things any differently. For me there are so many things I would do differently that I would dearly love to start farming all over again!

Chapter 9
From Generation to Generation

Since one cannot, alas, expect a second bite of the cherry, the significance of changes between the generations, if not fully shared, must at least be understood. It is probable that the best pointers on the road ahead lie not so much in the new developments that are in the pipeline as in people and the hopes they cherish. Generation succeeds generation, and the passing years can measure the progress made. Human nature being what it is, even the advent of computers does not materially change the terms in which we measure human society. Great literature and art succeed in spanning the centuries, and contribute to our sense of eternity, even in the face of doom-ladened prophecy. Dr Grigori Pomerants, a philosopher in present day Russia, records his view that Russia has lost her sense of eternity. It has been dislocated by the long communist interregnum. For him, it is the end of an era, a moment when the busy spirit of Martha must give way to the more contemplative spirit of Mary. But whatever the truth of his diagnosis, each new generation seeks its vision, and today we are perhaps beginning to be more concerned with the fundamentals of a satisfying way of life than the trappings of a successful career.

But for the moment many old certainties are called in question, and long dynasties may be interrupted and broken. Japan has perhaps the most expensively-supported agriculture in the world. A majority of her farmers have a pocket handkerchief of land, and could not live off it. But I shall always remember how one such farmer, asked how long his family had been farming this particular land, replied simply, '700 years'. He spoke without hesitation and without batting an eyelid. Is it necessarily progress to see such plots swallowed by city skyscrapers, albeit for a tidy sum in cash? This is not to say it should never happen, but progress also has to be in people as much as in modern infrastructure, as the current decay of our inner cities bears witness. It seems incongruous that buildings put up in living memory as part of a hopeful new development, should now be under demolition as vandalised slums. Moreover, our arrival in Japan coincided with the opening of Narita airport, under serious threat from determined farmer opposition. Today that same opposition is delaying a further extension.

In the course of the years, we have had over one hundred students staying with us and helping on the farm, as well as many visiting farmers from other countries. Some came to learn farming, some to learn English, and some hoped to do both. We have many happy memories, and have learnt a great deal from knowing them. Most came from Europe, and of course many from France, because of the varied links I had already forged there, and which feature in a later chapter. Needless to say, Kristin's cooking was widely appreciated, and her care helped them quickly to feel at home with us.

Browsing through past letters, I have made a series of extracts, which reflect some of the paths they have travelled after leaving. We try to keep in touch with as many as possible, and to know how they have fared, whether in farming themselves or in other jobs. It has also been a great joy on occasions to be able to meet their families, and in some cases even grown-up children. I have not identified the letter writers, but give the country and the date on the letter.

> I think it was me to whom the Conference (Farmers' meeting coinciding with a visit to the Royal Show at Stoneleigh) has been most interest, because I met for the first time people from Moral Re-Armament. I came to you when I knew only little about these ideas. I came without prejudice, nor good ones nor bad ones, and first time I have been surprised seeing people out of whole Europe who wanted to change their own nature, and that of mankind... Although I am concerned by the need of your ideas, I must tell you that I didn't yet find the courage to change myself. But I hope to succeed in time.
>
> HW, Germany, 18.8.65

In July I had such a great quarrel with my father that I took my suitcase immediately and went off. Since that time I picked up different jobs such as lorry driver etc. to earn much money and now I am studying at the University of Darenstadt... My parents agree with me that it is best for both sides to let the son go and study. It is still a cold atmosphere between us, but I am sure we will overwhelm that too.

HW, Germany, 5.11.67

The quarrels with my parents are really eliminated. I went home at Christmas, and we had a nice and lucky time together. Both parents agree in my studies and in my wish to go abroad to work in the developing countries.

HW, January 1968

Thank you for the welcome we had in England. It was marvellous and words can't express all we have felt in our hearts. Despite the very tough negotiations that are taking place in Brussels, and particularly the points which bring us into confrontation with England, we feel that during these days we have established links which can not be broken. It is no small result.

GB, France, 10.4.77

I am uneasy to see our President (FNSEA) speak very harshly about England. Once again the French farmers charge you with being at the bottom of all the troubles. Many demand the exclusion of England from the Common Market. Will the relations between our two peoples always be so finely balanced?

M Danguy keeps me regularly in touch with the initiatives of Moral Re-Armament. This winter I have been able to meet three of your English friends who are trying to keep their factory alive. I hope that their efforts are making headway?

GB, 20.2.89

I think much of you both at Longlands Farm and its working atmosphere, sometimes also of its ideas that I have never entirely accepted. What can you expect, we have thick (Bernois) heads, and on top of that a Swiss Romand character... I wish to do at least two years in Australia or New Zealand, countries which still offer good opportunities for learning and earning. But I wish first to do an English course in London before leaving.

As to the real future, I only see it in sombre colours, lightened by a few rosy touches, hours that I share with a wonderful girl. Of marriage and all the rest I don't even dare to think. As I am only twenty-two why ask oneself too many questions? But I don't truly conceive life in this vein. I hope one day to find the good road with or without God's help. Could you send me more news of Longlands farm? But only please as long as it doesn't mean you failing to have an evening's relaxation. Simpler perhaps to send me some photographs and I will return them.

CS, Switzerland, 29.10.73

We thank you warmly for your kindness and affectionate messages for our marriage, which has been one of the very positive events of the year 1979. The fire at our home on July 9th stirred up many emotions, but the help of friends locally has been wonderful, and we are immensely grateful for it. We have only been able to save the calves and the milking machines. It represents the turning of a page, with all the memories that go with it. This trial teaches us to be detached from material possessions. I hope you are well. Here all are well, and morale is good despite all the extra work caused by the construction of new buildings.

EC, Switzerland, 4.1.80

Many thanks for your letter, Pat. Am I right that you was in India on a international conference about development in industry and agriculture etc to help India out of its bad problems?

Afterwards you visited some projects, right? The text was a bit difficult for me but a good exercise. You've to know that my last English lesson is nearly one year ago. But it's good that not all people from Europe, Asia or from somewhere else are incurious about the fate of the Third World. Also it's good that young Indians are fighting against the problems in their country. Many Germans think that the people in the newly developing countries only wait for the money from Europeans. They need our help but they don't wait for the initiative of Europe. (I hope you understand what I want to say.)

As perhaps you know my adjudication as farmer began last summer when I left Longlands. I've to learn two years on farms, each year one farm.

MS, Germany, 27.4.81

The next extract is from a young Welshman who accompanied Kristin and me on a visit to India at New Year, 1983.

Well here I am, back at home with a somewhat distant memory of India. For my first two days in London I couldn't stop talking about the things I'd seen, but now I'm preparing to go to Scotland for seven months which is such a far remove from the sapping heat, and the lack of toast and jam.

My trip, however, wouldn't have been possible without your kind invitation to accompany you, and I would like to thank you both heartily for making the trip as pleasant as one can in such circumstances. Personally I found it an invaluable experience, and feel very privileged to have visited such a wonderful country while I am still a mere youngster. It was the friendly spirit and feeling that someone was going out of their way to help, which I found throughout my stay in India. After meeting such a dedicated man as Arun Chavan, who has devoted the best part of his life to making less fortunate and uneducated people's lives more than just a sense of survival, one sees he has done it by total unselfishness and disregard of personal status and material gain. Then one realises what power a man can be charged with when he listens to God.

SGP, Wales, 2.2.83

When I look back to the past time I'm very thankful and happy about the three months I spend in Longlands… Thank you for the openness to talk about everything and also trying to help me to find my way… The meetings with different people of the MRA (Moral Re-Armament) challenged my own faith, and made me think more in a way I often forget – responsibility for the other in my profession, and to think more about my neighbour wherever he is. What I'm very happy about and I'm hoping to help me in the coming time is the experience with Quiet Time. God is speaking and wants to talk to men if they listen. I know that I've to learn very much more on this point – not to collect thoughts and to measure the quality of my quiet time by the number of them etc – therefore I'm glad to have had the possibility to share the guidance each morning with you.

MH, Germany, 10.9.81

The last two weeks we were very busy with harvesting our potatoes, and doing all the other jobs necessary in the autumn like ploughing, drilling and so. I am happy to say that my thinking back is now not sad, but I've learnt something. For instance not to have such a good meaning of my own faith and way to live but to be humble. Also I had the thought to start to share the guidance with my parents. But what I am very happy about is what I learnt and recognised from the Quiet Time.

MH, 25.9.81

After University I'll start a year of experiencing different countries, firstly France to learn the language… It is not my wish and aim to become a good normal citizen – a lovely wife, two children,

8 hours work a day, four weeks holiday in Spain and a nice oak coffin! To live different means to fight, also to obey where God's offers are.

GH, Germany, 9.5.82

My unemployment depressed me in the last weeks. I lost my sense of being valuable and needed. It came like a disease. So I decided to continue my tropical studies at the University – (40kms from here) to keep myself informed about agriculture, and to prepare our plan to work in Africa.

GH, Germany, 13.8.85

I've applied for a job as technical officer with the local administration. More and more we have problems with nitrates in ground water. So the Government of Bad Wurttemberg has initiated a three year field study to find figures for maximum levels of nitrogen fertiliser that can be used with safe levels of nitrate in the drinking water. Eleven farmers are chosen to make test plots with different levels of organic and inorganic fertilisers. My task would be to organise and evaluate the trials and their results.

GH, 6.3.88

Just a kick from a cow in the milking parlour and I stayed one week in hospital... A kick of God to have a reflection on my life... The first years in this farm were hard, fairly hard, because the 1983 situation was bad. We have progressed quite fast in the past two years with God's help. Probably too fast for a balanced life. Its time to have a pause. Thanks for the daily habit I took in Longlands to consult God, to listen to Him. This was a precious help in the last seven years. But it's not enough regular...

EDB, France, 11.3.87

What does all this tell us about today? Mainly, perhaps, that the deepest need is to find faith and purpose in life. For the young, this comes before economics, though they do want to know how to make a living. Beyond that, a great many also seek a vision for their country and the world, and this should be a fundamental consideration in making fresh policy. More than ever, there will be pressure to try and get things right on a global scale.

The passage of the years may not make the good road easier to find and follow, but it is helpful to be linked in a wider purpose. This is enhanced by the rapid advance in communications, and the many manifestations that we are one world. It is increasingly possible to think of the world as a whole, with at least a measure of realistic understanding. So it is for this reason among others that Kristin and I cherish the opportunities to keep in touch with as many as possible of those who have visited the farm, and to share in what they are feeling and thinking. That is a farmers' network which, hopefully, will be increasingly influential in the future, ensuring that, on whatever scale we may have to organise, the individual will not go to the wall.

That is not to say that the number of farmers will not continue to diminish, but that we can be led to find what is right in the conflicting circumstances of the day. There may be a short-term inevitability in the course on which we are set, but in the longer term fresh perspectives can be established. Unless full employment becomes a feature of the urban scene, rural communities must find new life and the powerful motor of agriculture begin firing again on all cylinders. This is true not only for what it has to offer economically but also spiritually, because it is a mistake to see country life as a backwater, which is somehow out of date. That is essentially a Western perspective, and a false one, so it is in the countries where farming is still the dominant activity that fresh thinking may grow fastest.

Certainly, the question of career prospects for young people graduating from agricultural colleges is a vital one in many countries of Asia and Africa, and probably elsewhere. It is, I suppose, a fairly general experience that the majority of college graduates go into jobs with agro-industry or become researchers and administrators. In Thailand, where we have farming friends, there are some 54 agricultural colleges, and about 12% of their graduates are reckoned to become farmers themselves. This is a sufficient number to have a potentially important impact on the farming scene, and my own concern has been to see whether they get the backup and support which they feel they need. But although efforts are made from various quarters, so far there seems to be something lacking overall.

Here again it may be a lack of vision. It is a commonplace that at one time such graduates were looking for a collar-and-tie office job, and were frequently surprised to find their European or American counterparts getting their hands dirty on the farm. But by the same token, many such Western farmers would probably doubt that a 10-15 acre farm provided worthwhile scope for an educated farmer. In this I think they could be mistaken, partly because of the greater possibilities a tropical climate offers, and partly because graduate farmers will be the pioneers of an organic growth in society which can only come from within the community itself. It cannot credibly be organised by government, though government can certainly be a partner. But more importantly, it will come out of a growing professional status, and a transformation in social attitudes, with the realisation that getting richer is not a process that can in itself sustain society. Over the centuries, many farmers may not have got vastly richer, but they have accumulated a wealth of experience in the creation of communities.

In fact 'family farming' has become almost a synonym for the way of life embodied in farming. The farms here may be getting bigger but the concept remains the same, while elsewhere, extended families may create another kind of pressure for more land. But the important point is the quality of life which can be developed. In the spring of 1995, our local farmers' group, which operates under the flag of British Farmers for International Development (BFID) received two students of Animal Science from Chiangmai University in Thailand for a period of two months. Their lecturer in Animal Nutrition sent them because she felt they could find a wider horizon and an aim for life. It has been an initiative which looks likely to develop further. On the technical level, dairying is of particular interest to them, because Thailand has only had a dairy industry for the last thirty years. They have had no tradition of milking cows, but a booming economy has brought a rapid increase in the imports of dairy products. Now they are anxious to make up for lost time, while they are also, of course, deeply involved in pigs and poultry.

However, the meeting of two cultures has probably had more significance than what has been learnt technically. The Thais were experiencing their first journey outside their own country, while local farmers were chary of strangers who looked so slight and ill-equipped for farm-work here. In the event, the links made in the space of a few weeks seem to show it is a road worth pursuing, and one which will help to provide answers to some of the questions posed for future international relations and trade.

Kristin and I do not have children, much as we would like to have had. So, in a measure, the many young people who have come to stay are part of the family. We share a belief that everyone who crosses the threshold is someone we can learn to care for together. From that belief has come the conviction that home and the world could be one. Over the years, this has deepened into a purpose we shall always share. This doesn't mean that we are never critical of each other or do not approach many problems from opposite ends of the spectrum. Yet it does make it easier for us to relate the personal changes we both need to the greater goals we hope to reach. Personal change is very much more than simply becoming easier to live with. It is the measure of a commitment to God's will which builds a bridge between our lives and the lives of nations.

That is something worth weighing up, as one generation succeeds another. In these long-lived times, grandparents and even great grandparents may overlap, but there is no gap which cannot be bridged. It has become too easy and also too readily accepted that we walk out on problems instead of sticking with them. There is a continuity to be won in human relations that reflects the true potential of humanity. Now may be the moment to learn the terms on which such a continuity could be realised.

Chapter 10
Political Perspectives

Whatever our expectations of continuity, it is perhaps too much to hope that agriculture can occupy a realm above party politics. At the same time, it has usually enjoyed some consensus and common ground between the parties. It might even prove the policy area which finally persuades politicians of the need for longer-term aims in all they do. Cheap food was the cornerstone of industrial economies such as the UK's before the Second World War. But it did not help the countries who exported the food to cherish their agriculture as the nation's breadwinner. At the start of the process, cities grew when surplus farm labour migrated to find work in industry. That option is no longer there. The unemployed or marginally employed congregate in shanty towns or slums, exacerbating urban problems often acute enough already. It is a moment when affluent countries should come to terms with the real cost of their food, and envisage a narrowing of the gap between industrial and agricultural wealth. It would involve a radical change in the way we organise our markets, and governments have shrunk from such a confrontation. Yet conceivably the present moves towards a progressive reduction in subsidies will uncover fresh facts for public attention, and lead in that direction.

The attractions of a free market are great, but so long as that freedom is not absolute it must be hedged by qualification. Already, the centres of the textile industry have passed from one country to another, as the rise in wages and living standards has demanded a shift in the industrial base to a more remunerative field. It might be taken as the natural evolution in a competitive world, if the social dislocation involved had not been so great and even cruel. Dr Schumacher, in *Small is Beautiful*, examines the thesis that all food should be bought from where it is most cheaply produced. This is said to result both in higher income for agriculture and lower costs for the entire economy, particularly for industry. So no justification can be found for agricultural protectionism. He comments, 'If this were so, it would be totally incomprehensible that agricultural protectionism, throughout history, has been the rule rather than the exception. Why are most countries, most of the time, unwilling to gain these splendid rewards from so simple a prescription?' So perhaps it is worth examining the basic considerations which have governed farm policies in this century.

One of the pillars of European policy has been food security. This is the need to have basic home-grown supplies of food in the event of war, blockade or dislocation of supplies. The kind of publicity given to the so-called food mountains and the excesses of the CAP have devalued these considerations in the popular mind. But it is important to remember that they are also linked to questions of the stewardship of the countryside. A certain degree of self-sufficiency and support in the home market is basic to every agriculture, whether or not it is blessed with an amenable climate. To rule it out would be to destroy part of a country's essential physical presence and personality. It would be hard to conceive a country without any agriculture, though I once met a political leader from Namibia who, in reply to my enquiry about Namibian farming, said it didn't have any. He may have been correct within his personal terms of reference but, although it is known for its diamonds and minerals, the main primary products noted in my world atlas include cattle, sheep, maize and sorghum. Stock rearing and food processing even appear among its major industries.

The World Food Conference at Rome in 1974 was called on the basis of serious apprehension for world food supplies. For the first time perhaps, the activities of NGOs (Non Governmental Organisations), although outside the main flow of the Conference, did more than Governments to publicise the issues. Their initiatives tended to catch the imagination, whether in persuading gardeners and golf course managers to forgo the use of fertiliser in Pennsylvania or well-wishers to think of eating less meat to release more food grains for the hungry. That such initiatives were sometimes more well-intentioned than well-informed is in one sense beside the point. They sprang from a sincere motivation to meet a need, and they mobilised people to act. It is the political leaders, with their access to the levers of power, who could have translated these efforts into effective and well-judged action. But it is clear with hindsight that, after coming close to getting to grips with things, governments fumbled the ball and let play make its own way to the other end of the field. As a result, there is still a debate about the challenge to keep food production ahead of population growth but, in terms of current balances, there has been little fundamental change.

The great issues at Rome slipped through our fingers. No resolution was finalised on the maintenance of reserve stocks of food to meet future world needs. Rather, it was left for the marketplace to take over, when governments were unwilling to shoulder the responsibility. Many of the present insights on development issues seem still to have been a world away. Any thought of new global perspectives, such as those expressed by the Algerians, were rated as premature if not downright undesirable. Whether the disasters were natural or man-made, there was a lack of any official generosity of spirit in meeting them.

But when there was an earthquake at Tangshan in China two years later, international offers of help were forthcoming. Unfortunately, the Chinese Government had set its face against accepting such aid. I reflected on this recently when a leader from Tangshan expressed her mystification at this refusal. She was at the heart of the heroic efforts to meet the crisis and, later, to rebuild. She expressed her appreciation of the Central Government's help, but had questioned their attitude in excluding the international community. I remembered the Chinese delegates at the Rome Conference, in their blue Mao uniforms, who had seemed so difficult to approach. Even a traditional opening on the subject of the weather did not get very far! It had seemed at the time, and evidently correctly, that the difficulty arose more from ideology than from language.

Now, however, things have changed and, though the difficulties are as great as ever, there is fresh hope abroad for the role of the United Nations. Too many of the food crises in Africa and elsewhere have been occasioned by civil war and the breakdown of government. Changes of attitude in member states have opened the way to better teamwork, but its achievement is far from automatically guaranteed. There is much to admire in the goodwill and conviction shown by UN troops in the former Yugoslavia as they attempted, sometimes under fire, to alleviate the worst of war's horrors. But they deserve to be deployed with more foresight and preparation, rather than thrust in only when things have got out of control.

So far as the food arm of the UN is concerned, it has to be said that the FAO (Food and Agriculture Organisation) has been something of a disappointment. It has assembled a massive amount of information and statistics, but it has signally failed to mobilise the passion of committed agriculturalists and farmers, or to empower them to break through the bureaucracy. But the rise of the NGOs, sometimes in fruitful partnership with government, has multiplied the alternative options.

There are still important arguments over the role of transnational companies and the development of subsistence economics into agricultural export. Nearly everyone will respond positively to the slogan 'Better trade than aid', but it begs the question of what may be involved in the terms of trade. That, more than anything, is the sticking point for Agriculture. The long-drawn-out agonies of the recent GATT (General Agreement on Tariffs and Trade) negotiations are but one illustration, and it is impossible to pretend that answers have yet been found. Everything depends on the nature of the World Trade Organisation which has just come into being. Sir Leon Brittan has said that the WTO will substitute the rule of law for the rule of the jungle. It is much to be hoped that that is true, but it will have to go even further if it is to link free trade with fair trade. So far, such a concept has been beyond GATT's remit, but perhaps the inclusion of agriculture can herald a change of perspective.

In fact, moving from questions of food security to the sharing of abundance is proving unusually fraught for the governments of affluent countries. The pressures may often be expressed in arguments over economic theory, but they are far more fundamentally a challenge to temper enterprise with unselfishness. Even with a genuine desire to help, it is hard to come to terms with the fact that the problems of feeding a hungry world will not be answered simply by producing more. Nor is it true that our job is to stand aside and open our markets on the assumption that the benefit will be reaped by those in need of it. It is not a question of supply and demand, but a question of motivation. Those who call for a change in lifestyle may be quite right but, unless they can define that change in moral and spiritual terms, they may fail to convince. As with so many advocates of birth control, they have their eyes on practical and mathematical targets, rather than on the creative forces in society.

Strangely enough, we may now be nearer to admitting that human wisdom has failed than we have been for a long time. Ted Heath is credited with coining the phrase 'the unacceptable face of capitalism', and it is one which lingers and will require an answer. That answer may not come quickly, because it is part of finding a cure for a sick society, but the failure of communism only makes the need more acute. That need is mirrored in Oliver Walston's parable of the West German farmer who took over the land of a bankrupt Cooperative in the East.

I was told about a famous Schleswig-Holstein arable farmer who, seeing the opportunities in the East, last autumn drove east and found a bankrupt Cooperative farm. In the best traditions of Western business, he made them an offer they couldn't refuse. So while most of his neighbours back home were still trying to put together their own deals and locate the small landowners necessary for the process, this particular farmer got down to work.

After ploughing and drilling the home farm, he led a convoy of his own tractors eastwards, and eventually reached the newly rented land. The Wessis, equipped with the latest in tractor technology, set to work on the huge eastern fields. The Ossis were not amused.

To the farmer himself it probably looked like the ultimate triumph of capitalism over the discredited collective system of agriculture. And in a sense it was. But the price was high. One morning his tractor driver arrived for work to find that the tyres had been slashed, the hydraulic pipes cut and the windows smashed. Not long afterwards the farmer suffered a heart attack.

(*Farmer's Weekly*, May 1991)

Such a story makes its own point that social as well as economic considerations enter in. Similar reactions to the workings of capitalism convinced Karl Marx that economics were all important to the human condition. The message may be that both capitalism and communism have got it wrong without a moral and spiritual foundation. That is why environmental considerations and the access of the public to the countryside, though complicating the picture economically, are raising the question of a moral and spiritual dimension. The idea of the quality of life is involved, and it seems that many city dwellers instinctively feel that nature has something to contribute. It is for that reason that they are ready as taxpayers to make some contribution to the support of a viable rural community. If we want to reshape agricultural policy, then we must bid to retain that support and develop better understanding of the real issues.

Common Agricultural Policy reform is but a very temporary stepping stone. It needs to be rethought from the beginning as M Pisani argued in a powerful article in *Le Monde* (May 1992). He wrote of the need to work out an international strategy for agricultural development, balanced nutrition and environmental conservation. He envisaged a five-yearly review of such a strategy undertaken by all those interests concerned, so that the agricultural world should become wholly responsible for its own destiny. But he drew attention to the differences of philosophy between the USA and Europe, which need to be debated first, and which need to focus on the kind of agriculture we want, rather than simply focusing on fulfilling market requirements.

All of this would break new ground by making policy in a world context. The North American Free Trade Area (NAFTA) was launched chiefly as an economic initiative. But it, too, will have to come to grips with social and environmental considerations. I was struck by the view of a Canadian friend that much of the pressure in the US for a North American alliance arose because they felt threatened by the emergence of the European Union as a trading bloc. We are perhaps too prone to underestimate our own power and to be unaware of what may lie behind sometimes seemingly abrasive American attitudes. It is always easier to establish understanding farmer to farmer but, having done that, we must take the next step into the realms of government. Working with government has become an essential exercise for farmers worldwide, and there can be no turning back. For all the understandable wish in the farming community to minimise government interference in production, there will always need to be consultation over the grand strategy.

In this connection, large trading blocs can perhaps ease the task of inter-continental consultation. I well remember hearing African diplomats from English-speaking countries saying how well they had got to know their French-speaking colleagues in the course of the Lome negotiations. Lome called for an African view on questions of agricultural trade, and this meant crossing barriers of language and custom as well as the sometimes arbitrarily drawn frontiers. Similar efforts for regional coordination are at work in Latin America and South East Asia, and it sometimes amazes me to think how recent the whole process in Brussels really is. It has become fashionable to rail against the bureaucracy there, but the reality is modest beside our individual national agriculture ministries. The farming bureaucracy in Whitehall still outnumbers Brussels despite the vast amount of work caused by the need for translation into many languages.

However, the advent of three new countries highlighted the unwieldy nature of an enlarged Commission where the same field of work has now to be shared among a larger number of Commissioners. But changes in structure are forced by circumstances just as they have been in farming itself. The bigger question is how enlargement underlines the need for greater simplicity, and the detailed interpretation of that now famous principle of 'subsidiarity'. Paradoxically, decentralisation remains a key principle in allowing greater cohesion on a world scale. But there would seem to be no way round increased majority voting and greater powers for the European Parliament as essential steps on the road forward.

Suffice it to say for the moment that political perspectives may have to change on quite a fundamental level. It is only human to look for familiar ways, and to hope to establish a dominant pattern in the areas of main concern. But with the US as the last 'officially remaining superpower', it is perhaps a good moment to look at the possibility of a new era. Could it be that power will no longer reside in the big battalions, and that genuine consensus will be more highly prized?

Whatever the answer, it is certain that, more and more, people will want to choose their own paths in life, and that, more and more, government will be judged on its ability to deliver the chance to choose. It seems likely to follow from this that smaller countries will see their influence grow rather than diminish, and that regional groupings will have to find their unity in teamwork born of a common purpose. That common purpose will have to grow out of shared values forged in today's world rather than relying simply on past heritage. William Blake is not exactly everyone's favourite visionary, but he may have struck one of his prophetic notes when he wrote, 'Religion and politics – are they not the same thing?'

Certainly, both are concerned with man's destiny on earth, and the creation of a just society. For many years, moreover, Blake's vision of Jerusalem in England's green and pleasant land has been the theme song of the Women's Institutes. It has reverberated through a national organisation which has been a bastion of rural society during most of the twentieth century. Although dubbed 'Jam and Jerusalem' by the teasingly cynical, the WI has reflected an essentially Christian view of the rural way of life. 'Thy will be done on earth' remains a commitment to the world's affairs, which could still have the power to regenerate political faith in the next century.

Tony Blair's new Labour Party may not yet have claimed that birthright, but it certainly lived in Labour's first parliamentarian, Keir Hardie. Even more strikingly, Blake's contemporary, William Wilberforce, was dubbed 'God's politician', and devoted himself to revolutionising the political attitudes of the day. Unusual in not seeking government positions which he could easily have had, he has still left his mark on history. His career demonstrates the essential link between private life and the service of country. It has no theocratic implications, for Blake, when he spoke of religion, did not think in institutional terms. He meant the purity of the inward vision and the quality of leadership to which it gives rise.

Chapter 11
People and Policies

Wisely, the NFU has always had a non-party political stance, even though it has been popularly supposed, and probably rightly, that the majority of farmers vote Conservative. It could be claimed that there is a quality of common sense in the farming community which reacts to the excesses of party bias and clings to the practical points needed for a settlement of immediate issues. Certainly, that was true of the leadership of James Turner and Kenneth Knowles in the immediate post war years. They made the NFU a power in the land, and established a tradition which has only faltered recently. As already noted, Turner went further with the founding of the International Federation for Agricultural Producers (IFAP) and, as Lord Netherthorpe, taking up a major role in industry through companies such as Fisons and Lloyds Bank, while also contributing immensely to the enlargement of the role of the Royal Agricultural Society of England (RASE) with its permanent base at Stoneleigh.

Looking back to the days when we were contemplating entry to the European Union, it is interesting to read the proceedings of the meeting convened on the subject by the Farmers' Club, which gathered 1200 of us at the Friends Meeting House in November 1962. The morning session was addressed by Ted Heath, then negotiating the possible terms for British entry. He spoke for over an hour without notes, and it was a considerable *tour de force.* In the afternoon, a discussion was prefaced by speeches from Tristram Beresford, Wiltshire farmer and Agricultural Editor of the *Financial Times*, and Asher Winegarten, Chief Economist and later also Director General of the NFU. Quite apart from the high level of interest aroused, it was evident even then that people tended to divide on the basis of their faith in the future rather than the balance of present realities, where comparisons were not easily made.

Beresford spoke on the basis of harder times ahead for farming and the 'balance of disadvantage'. This led him to favour participation in Europe, and it is interesting to note that he identified the disposal of surpluses as being the great headache of 'industrial agriculture'. But he felt, understandably enough, that their disposal might be easier if we were part of a Common Market! Winegarten, though perceived by many as against going in, was at pains to establish his objectivity. He tended to count those for as the optimists, and those against as the pessimists. But he strove manfully to extract figures which would provide an assessment of what was involved in cash terms. He was rightly determined that farmers should go forward with their eyes open.

Even at the grass-roots, the same interest was evident, and some years later the subject attracted the biggest attendance in living memory at our Bromyard local branch of the NFU. Happily, by this time, the NFU had found a leader matched to the hour in Henry Plumb. Convinced of his cause, he was close enough to the daily round of farming to take care of the worries of the working farmer. He inspired trust, whatever doubts may have been harboured about European rhetoric and ideological principles. In fact, it was during his Presidency of the Union that the biggest national protest ever staged took place, in an effort to inform the public of the dangerous economic effects of the squeeze being put on agriculture. Only a few years later, we joined the European Community, and Henry Plumb's subsequent career in the European Parliament has amply demonstrated the integrity of his commitment.

It is interesting to note that, in a parallel way, several French farmers' leaders also became members of the European Parliament, among them François Guillaume, Louis Lauga and Bernard Thareaux. But my own association with French farming goes back to 1948, when I worked for a few months on the farm of Philippe Schweisguth at Andrésy, near Pontoise. Paris, still pockmarked by bullets and with streets bearing plaques with the names of those gunned down on them, bore witness to the scars of war. It was my first concrete experience of how differently things may look from another vantage point.

Only recently, I heard for the first time a story of Philippe's intervention in a village dispute over women accused of consorting with the Germans during the occupation. In a mob action, several women had been manhandled and their hair cut off in retribution, when Philippe arrived on the scene. He at once sought a vantage point from which he could harangue the crowd, challenging the justice of their kangaroo court, and questioning what they really knew about the women they had condemned. One woman, whose head was still unshorn, he took under his protection and succeeded in saving from the fate which awaited her. It was an act of high courage in the circumstances of the day, when feelings ran high. So he was a man who was quick to stand up against mass emotion, though I know from my own observation how deeply he venerated the memory of Claire Girard, a young woman of the Resistance who was shot by German soldiers in a small wood we sometimes had occasion to pass.

Apart from such legacies of war, there was much else to get accustomed to in the daily round, from shovels and forks with long handles to long midday breaks and a late, late evening meal to end the day. Pierre Le Calvez, the horseman, was a happy-go-lucky character who would collect up the big snails in his handkerchief to bear home for a good feed. Little did I think then that snail farming would become one of the endless diversifications to appear in the UK! Among the 'stagiaires' (farm pupils) the dynamic Côme Alexandre was outstanding, but was later killed at his own farm in an accident on the silage clamp. Pere Manuel, the cowman from the Valle-D'Aosta, could not be communicated with easily. But if not a local, he was fully part of the team. Then there was Pere Carre, an old pensioner who had made his home on the farm and accomplished all sorts of minor jobs around the buildings and livestock. He would dispense home-made cider with many a wisecrack, which unfortunately too often escaped my understanding.

Philippe Schweisguth was active with a number of others in setting up *Le Journal de la France Agricole*, a weekly paper run by an independent group of farmers. It may seem surprising today, but at the beginning, the *France Agricole* was outgunned by the Communist Party with their paper *La Terre*. It was a dedicated band who saw it through those early years, and Board meetings were lively. On the only occasion I was present at one, my French was quite unequal to the cut and thrust of the discussion, but one could absorb the atmosphere and the spirit. Some spoke with passion, and all with an intensity and eagerness to articulate their ideas.

Today, it is the leading farm weekly in France and still in the hands of farmers, though of course staffed as always by professional journalists. Philippe died in 1993 when in his eighties, and right up to his death was still making his regular weekly contribution under the nom de plume of 'Le Cheval de Devant' (The Leading Horse). The brevity demanded by his allotted space took care and artistry to fulfil. But he rarely failed to conjure some deeper reflection from current and familiar topics. It was a unique combination of head and heart, which won the loyal support of countless readers, as their letters testified.

There is no doubt that the *France Agricole* has played an important part on the farming scene, which is so much more highly politicised than ours. The readiness of French farmers to take to the streets has become a byword, and militants in the NFU have frequently called for us to emulate them. No doubt, on occasion, they have secured concessions by their passion but, too often, they have acted in defiance of their official leaders. The brother of a friend of mine in Brittany has been permanently disabled by a gendarme's baton, when all he did was to go to see what was happening. Too many of the innocent fall victim, for such confrontations to produce long-term benefit. But the French have also been responsible for much more creative initiatives, most notably the movement for farmer-to-farmer links with overseas countries, Agriculteurs Français et Développement International (AFDI). Founded in 1975, it followed on from the collection of 5 million Francs by the French farming community to alleviate the effects of drought in the Sahel region, south of the Sahara desert. Having helped to assuage a famine caused by extreme drought, French farmers asked themselves how the African farmers' situation could be improved. They began to want to understand the whys and wherefores, and were no longer content with the effort simply to meet a crisis. Those in whom convictions were kindled at this point were not afraid to proclaim the need for farming solidarity on a world basis. As one document of the day noted, 'Farming solidarity doesn't have to stop at national or European level. It is not a sudden access of the urge to "do good" and follow a fashion of "helping the Third World", but a necessary continuation of an action which had been developing over almost a hundred years.'

AFDI declared itself open to all in the rural community interested in the realities of Third World development. Regional groups pursuing their own programmes gave it the chance to develop a variety of forms, and great emphasis was laid on farmer-to-farmer links as the starting point. When Louis Lauga (FNSEA, French Farmers Union) first suggested to me that something similar might be undertaken in Britain, I was particularly impressed with this emphasis. It was made clear that it was not a question of looking for a suitable project to back, but of going into a village or a district to live for several weeks and begin to understand the farming being practised. From that would come the opportunity to learn the aspirations of the farmers, and what they themselves saw as the way forward. There was no point in supplying any sort of machinery, whether tractor or pump, which could not be serviced and maintained locally. Development must come out of the will of the farmers involved, even if the pace of progress might seem slow to western eyes fixed on the size of the technology gap rather than the nature of the communities involved.

Despite the rapid increase in the possibilities of modern communication, the 'listening level' on development issues is described in a 1983 AFDI document as relatively feeble. That is why it was felt that farmer-to-farmer contact could be of particular importance, and that good organisation is no substitute for an understanding spirit. It is important to do one's homework on a situation thoroughly, but it is then necessary to experience the realities on the ground. The FNSEA (French Farmers' Union) in 1981 was commenting that a collective framework ought to constitute a way of expressing individual values, and not be an end in itself. They even went further, by mentioning the possible role of the Catholic Church in contributing to the effectiveness of an action which depends on the moral and spiritual foundations of an active faith.

At the same time, it was not long before AFDI became a surprisingly comprehensive organisation. It had a national structure which embraced the Farmers' Unions, the Chambers of Agriculture, the cooperatives and organisations for insurance and credit, but all functioning at a regional level. In this sense, French agriculture is far more cohesive than British agriculture, and is a great advantage when it comes to linking up a diversity of efforts which share a common overall purpose. Thus, in the development field, it facilitates the multiplication of direct links and contacts, which can operate both at government and non-government levels. Ultimately, too, it will fuse with the strengthening of indigenous farm organisations, a particular preoccupation of IFAP (International Federation of Agricultural Producers).

Although such organisation is a strength and, to some extent, a guarantee of further growth, it also has its pitfalls, particularly so if institutions are established too quickly and become rigid. They need to grow organically, and that is why decentralisation is so important. It is the pursuit of the spirit rather than the letter of the law which counts.

It is for this reason that the future of the European Parliament remains a matter of the greatest interest. In Britain, some have seen it as a stepping stone to Westminster, others as a liberation from parochial preoccupations, enabling them to grapple with history in the making. But while it is still in the full flow of evolution, and its future powers have still to be determined, its influence grows from the very much underestimated cross-fertilisation of ideas. In that sense, it is an ongoing forum which survives mockery and allegations of cushy jobs by opening the door to all who come knocking to seek help or advice. In a visit during 1992, I experienced for myself the welcome given to a party of four Polish farmers by a French MEP, while I was told that the chairman of the group (a British MEP) conducting a dialogue with them, finished by engaging them in a direct discussion in Russian.

What will grow in such a fertile seedbed remains to be seen. But that agriculture will play an important part in it is beyond doubt, if only because it is the field of activity most comprehensively integrated in the policies already developed. François Guillaume has put on record his own view of farming politics during his Presidency of the FNSEA. On the subject of French farmers' demonstrations against decisions taken in Brussels, he says, 'The multiplication of these conflicts in the bosom of French society prompts us to reflect on the way they are expressed and their results. Properly directed, they are a forceful part of the dialogue, but marginalised or even repressed they become a danger to democracy. The exercise of democracy cannot simply be expressed by casting a ballot at regular intervals. It needs the active participation of different social and professional bodies to elaborate and put into practice economic and social policies.' Later he observed, 'I know many of these civil servants, whether they are French or from other countries. They are men of quality, conscious of the important part they have to play in the building of Europe.'

Subsequently, François Guillaume found himself appointed Minister of Agriculture, where his restless drive sought to establish a legitimate field for the expansion of French and European agricultural exports. As he wrote of the heyday of the CAP's success, 'No one would have imagined that twenty five years after the Treaty of Rome, France would become second only to the United States as a leading exporter of agricultural and food products.' He conceived a plan which would have attempted to establish a true world market price for cereals, while using the money saved on subsidising exports to finance development in the Third World. It was a concept which required a very high degree of trust between the parties involved, and it is not surprising that it foundered when even friends were lukewarm. The General Secretary of IFAP said Guillaume was simply enunciating ideas which had already been put forward by his organisation. Such a verdict only underlined the fact that like many men of drive and ambition, Guillaume could on occasion be abrasive and impatient. Yet another case where the application of what's right rather than who's right might have saved the day. For there is no doubt that a substantial consensus could be found on this subject which would embrace all but the most ardent advocates of free play for market forces. Even the latter might become reluctant converts, because it is very evident today that simply negotiating tariff reductions is not the way forward. Greater opportunities must be afforded to the most disadvantaged.

An interesting sidelight on this was afforded at the World Food Conference organised by Lord Plumb at Brussels in the spring of 1988. In a session on development issues, where time was clearly going to be limited for all those who wished to speak, Guillaume, as Chairman, made a bid to limit the length of contributions. Since representatives of such august bodies as the World Bank and other international institutions had prepared papers which had been circulated, he suggested that they should limit their speeches to underlining main points, so that representatives from developing countries and NGOs would have a better chance to make their contributions. In the event, everyone read their papers in full, and totally ignored the Chairman's suggestion. Another opportunity lost to show the listening ear that is needed at every step.

But for other reasons, the occasion at Brussels in 1988 was by no means wasted. Lord Plumb has used his career as a European parliamentarian in a structured but flexible way to begin to shape a coherent course for world agriculture. The Brussels Conference was the first fruit of the International Policy Council on Agriculture and Trade established in 1987. It was followed by an East/West Conference in Budapest in October 1990, aimed at bringing into focus the issues raised by the collapse of communism and the need to develop both new economies and new relationships between peoples. These are small steps on a long road, but there is no doubt that current needs are serving to accelerate the pace. For a long time, international action has been viewed as at best visionary, at worst simply pie-in-the-sky. But whatever controversy may surround current UN initiatives in various parts of the world, it is clear that they are no longer without influence. Lord Plumb's Policy Council has become a constructive influence, and its unofficial status an advantage in generating new initiatives.

One thing the Brussels Conference of 1988 made clear was the ugliness of the confrontation building up between the US and the EU over the GATT negotiations. It was epitomised in remarks addressed by Mark Clinton (Irish MEP) to the American Secretary for Agriculture, Richard Lyng. At one point, Clinton even pointed an accusing finger, saying 'I am looking at you Mr Secretary.' This was in the context of those who say one thing and do another. Lyng was not to be drawn, and made no direct reply. But echoes of the Irish comments that day could be heard from the French farmers later.

I only became more acutely aware of this division myself when I was in Washington in April 1989. I was lunching with one of the US Trade Commissioners, and had referred to the kind of love/hate relationship which has existed through the years between the American Farm Bureau (the largest US farmers' organisation) and the IFAP. The Farm Bureau is a leading defender of free enterprise and the market economy. Though it has supplied several Presidents of IFAP, it has always felt a little out of step with the ethos of that organisation, and has sometimes left it, only subsequently to rejoin.

Even so, I was somewhat taken aback to be asked, 'Would you sit down with your enemies, and help to finance them?' It seemed a harsh judgement of the relations between fellow farmers, albeit competitors, but it throws light on the way the GATT negotiations subsequently dragged on without settlement. Indeed it would seem that Edgard Pisani was right when he called for a total rethink of the CAP. He wrote in *Le Monde*, 'We have to work out an international strategy for agricultural development, balanced nutrition and environmental conservation. GATT is certainly not the best forum in which to debate it, and to limit ourselves to the GATT debate is to go off on a false scent. It is to try and regulate through the market alone, processes which involve both nature and society. That is a short-sighted way to try and sort out the future of mankind.'

The kind of debate which Pisani advocated in 1992 has begun to develop not only in his Groupe de Seillac but in a number of different fora. The important thing is that these should not be simply gatherings of the like-minded, and that they should be truly international in character. Perceptions of the national interest may change in such a process. Certainly it will be a new day if the politicians involved can emerge with a common agenda which addresses the practical need of a strategy for world agriculture. It may lead us to ask whether we are colleagues or competitors, and whether there is a common purpose which lies beyond present preoccupations.

Chapter 12
Colleagues or Competitors

The development of the European Union has highlighted a situation in which farmers have become both colleagues and competitors. Before our entry, British farmers saw their fellows almost solely as colleagues uniting to get the best deal for farming. If there was competition, it was more to turn in a better performance that to capture another man's market. Looking over the hedge involved a competition to see who was first in drilling the wheat or sending in the combine harvester. Even the pleasure of boasting a top yield did not preclude sharing information on the methods employed. Launching a takeover bid for a neighbour in difficulties would have been unthinkable: rather, many would rally round to try and help him out of trouble.

There is still a sense of solidarity among the Community's farmers, but with nationalist undertones which inevitably become louder when the going gets tough. Yet although federalism may appear to be a political hot potato, in farming terms it is rather a red herring. Farmers are committed to working a common policy, and they understand that common institutions are bound to be federal in nature if they are to work at all. It involves a sacrifice of independence, but it does not involve a loss of national identity. The main point is to find a system that is fair for everyone.

This leads on to the famous argument about securing a level playing field. Chiefly it comes down to legislating a common system, but the letter of the law still needs the support of an enabling spirit. Certainly, if milk quotas are put in place, and one or more countries cannot comply till some years later, cohesion is bound to be weakened. But more insidious is the sniping which has traditionally gone on between the British and the French. Each side seems convinced that the other is pulling a fast one, with a superb cunning that goes undetected. Most of the time, this is a complete myth, but the love/hate relationship seems to persist. We may be understandably up in arms when lorry loads of British lamb carcases are put to the torch but, when the French take to the streets against GATT, envious British voices suggest we should be doing the same.

Suffice it to say that there is little danger of national character becoming submerged! Rather, we may have to face the fact that with government, as with climate, there is no such thing as a level playing field. So it is better to decide for what values we are prepared to go to the stake, and make them the founding principles of every policy. Some issues divide along national lines and some don't. But the principle of subsidiarity is expressly designed to reduce unnecessary conflict. It is here that common sense can be set free to tear out the red tape. Then, local arrangements can be made to supply rough cider or dubious-smelling cheeses, providing they meet a demand and are correctly labelled, without the need to monitor them at every stage and declare them up to European standards of hygiene.

Likewise, in international marketing, there may have to be a change of direction. In the dispute over grain markets in GATT, Europe was seen, rightly or wrongly, as having taken over markets which were traditionally American. In other areas, other perceptions may rule. Europe has introduced dairy quotas, and thereby lessened pressures on international markets, but it is unacceptable that world prices should be depressed by export subsidies, whatever their origin. Of course, in the first instance, such subsidies are granted to prevent excessive stocks but, further back, one has to examine how surpluses arise and then become a built-in part of the system. But since so many people passionately believe it is wrong to limit production when millions across the world are hungry, it is also necessary to study the shortages. Perhaps it is time for Europe and the United States to concentrate on these, rather than seeking to divide existing markets, thoughtless of the longer term. That means facing the fact that the decisions needed are political and not economic. For whether the underlying trend is towards surplus or shortage, a lack of purchasing power remains the real problem.

Some political changes in recent history have been examined by the Centre for Strategic and International Studies in Washington DC with a view to evaluating the role of moral and spiritual factors. One such change was the settlement which established the independence of Zimbabwe, and for me the story of one African farmer at that time has become symbolic for the whole continent. John Musekiwa farmed in the north close to the frontier near Mount Darwin, and his family memories included a great grandfather killed in the Zulu wars. As an ordinary farmer, his change of heart towards the conflict which had drifted into civil war showed that anyone can have a hand in history.

John's farm became a regular route for guerilla forces entering the country. He welcomed them and wished them well, but as time went on he was increasingly distressed to see young men lying dead in a struggle that seemed unending. Then he was arrested and imprisoned on suspicion of helping the guerillas. But, without proof, he was finally released. He met Arthur Kanodereka, a friend who had been marvellously freed from his hatred for the white man. Arthur was a Methodist minister, but he had supposed that the limit of his ministry was to the black people. He became instead a fearless fighter for a just peace.

John was puzzled and somewhat aghast at this radical turnaround in thinking. But it worked in his mind together with Arthur's conviction that God would speak to those who cared to listen, and show them what to do. He decided to confront the hatred in his own life by apologising to the District Officer who had been responsible for his arrest and imprisonment. It took him some time hanging around the office to pluck up his courage. But then he saw the District Officer entering and slipped quickly in behind him. When the man reached his office and turned round he was astonished to find John standing there. John told him what he had come to say, and turned to leave with the District Officer literally speechless. However the man found his voice at last, and said, 'Perhaps I should have been the one to apologise to you.'

That experience convinced John that he should get behind the efforts for a settlement. When the election was organised, he went out into the bush to persuade the guerilla fighters to come in to vote. Often they were so distrustful that he took his life in his hands, and did not know whether he would be released to go further. But the elections were held, and Robert Mugabe was returned with a triumphant majority.

Then John set about helping some of the guerilla fighters to get back into farming. After years of fighting and living off other people's work, it was not an easy transition to make. John had the only tractor in his district, and he decided to use it for his own farm four days a week and work for others two days a week. This he did on a contract basis, planning to be paid when the crop came to harvest. But for those whom he judged unable to do this, he waived payment altogether. With the backing of government policy, the success story of the small African farmers in Zimbabwe is now well known. But it was the dedication of men like John Musekiwa which helped push things forward.

Then another human column began to take the track through John's farm, refugees from Mozambique. He came home one day to find a large cooking pot on the fire, and a number of refugees gathered. His wife told him that she felt God meant them to do all they could for these people in need. From that day, John's farm was a support to all who passed through in their flight from Mozambique; and some who were too weak to go on stayed to be fed and nursed back to health. When we think of African farmers, we do not often remember the basic work of families like the Musekiwas, living proof that ordinary farmers can have a part in reshaping society, and in influencing the course of history.

I have dwelt on this experience because it is at the heart of the great issues of our time, the gap between the rich and poor countries and the spread of democracy in the political life of nations. In speaking of democracy, it may be necessary to make clear that it is not just some western style of government that is meant, but the chance for people to participate in freedom and with conviction, whether they represent a minority or majority interest.

In the days of the Communist Empire, people often mistakenly saw the battle lines as drawn only between countries. Today it is clearer than ever that the battle is fought in people's hearts across all frontiers and cultures. Nationalism may be having a resurgence mainly as a reaction to insecurity. We try to defend our own corner which is known to us and which is dear to us, but we do not advance our cause by attacking others. This was brought home to me during the Falklands/Malvinas War, when I received a letter from Celedonio Pereda, President of the Sociedad Rural, one of Argentina's main farm organisations. It was in reply to a letter I had written him, and I found it very moving, the more so perhaps because it was written on the day of the Argentine surrender.

> I received today your letter dated May 31st, for which I am very grateful. In a very clear and relevant way you put forward your ideas on the very old conflict, whose history is generally unknown, and which has brought along this unbelievable situation between our two countries (I would say our two governments more than our two countries) which is totally unnecessary, absolutely outdated, unrealistic and maybe too conveniently used here and there for internal political consumption.

> After today's news we will certainly have to begin to construct bridges, rethink solutions and correct failures we both have been incurred in. As you very well express, we farmers can and will find ways to continue to work together in that process of making and restoring peace and good will between our countries. Your reference to the Pope's visit to your country is moving, and his visit here with practically no time to prepare it, has attracted millions and made a unique impression on our people, specially the young.

> Maybe after all we can hope for better co-operation and understanding.

Unfortunately, Pereda died in a road accident only a few months after writing this letter. But it has remained for me a guiding light in the process of healing and reconciliation which has now begun. It has been symbolised in the meeting between Horacio Benitez, a 19-year-old Argentine conscript left for dead with horrific head wounds, and Major Chris Keeble, who took over command of the 2nd Parachute Battalion on the death of Lt Colonel H Jones. Indeed, for all the efforts to recreate the atmosphere of the war on television, this remains for me the outstanding reality in retrospect, of a reconciliation forged between opponents in the conflict, and the vision of a forward road in place of confusion worse confounded. The kernel of the story is worth giving as it was reported by Michael Smith in the magazine *For A Change* (April/May 1992).

> Suddenly the words that Chris Keeble will never forget crackled through on his radio: 'Sunray is down'. Their Commanding Officer Lt Colonel H Jones was dead – killed in action as he stormed an Argentine gun position.
>
> As second in command, Keeble took charge of 400 men. 'My heart beat faster. It was a tremendous responsibility.' By nightfall, 2 Para was running out of ammunition. 'We had been fighting for 40 hours and we were very tired. It was bitterly cold. One in six of us was either injured or killed, and we had no reinforcements. I went back to my group of leaders and it was clear that they were looking to me for solutions.
>
> 'We were in a perilous position, and the responsibility for getting us out of it lay with me. I had no idea what to do. I walked up a gully to be alone for a moment to try and think. I put my hands in my pockets and my fingernails caught on a piece of plastic. It was a prayer which I had typed out and had laminated as a kind of deal with God – you know – "I'll carry this prayer if you'll look after me" stuff.'
>
> Keeble knelt in the gorse and said this prayer. 'My Father, I abandon myself to you. Do with me as you will. Whatever you

may do with me I thank you, providing your will is fulfilled in me. I ask for nothing more.' He found it in the midst of battle, 'a terrifying, almost impossible prayer to say. But to my amazement I went through a real transformation. Instead of feeling frightened, uncertain, cold, miserable, confused, I suddenly felt joyful, happy, warm.'

Above all, he had 'immense clarity' about what he needed to do. He returned to his men and told them that at first light he would walk down across the battlefield and invite the Argentine commanders to surrender. His men were 'pretty astounded by this very unmilitary kind of solution. We were a unit that was designed to bring violence to produce a solution and I was offering one that was completely the reverse.'

At 6.00am Keeble returned two Argentine prisoners to their commanders with a stark message: 'Surrender or accept the consequences of military action'. The commanders were ready to talk and by midday had agreed to surrender with dignity. They held a formal parade, sang their national anthem and laid down their arms. 'I think that is what was most significant', said Keeble. 'I was offering them something that they wanted anyway. But I could not have known that when I said that prayer...'

In July 1987, shortly before he left the army, Keeble received a phone call from an army padre. Would he be willing to receive an Argentine war veteran who was on a personal mission to the UK seeking reconciliation and forgiveness? Horacio Benitez, a 19 year old conscript during the war, had ended up with a bullet in his skull. But he also had traumatic memories of emptying two machine gun magazines into advancing British soldiers. 'You ask yourself how many fathers you may have killed. And you ask yourself why?' he told *The Guardian* (London). Now he wanted to seek out those in the British military to whom he could express his regret. The Ministry of Defence declined, but Keeble responded.

In the *Guardian* interview, Benitez described their encounter.

'It was very important for me to meet Chris. I was very worried. I didn't know what he would think, meeting me "the enemy". But he just held out his hand, then embraced me. It was so emotional I couldn't speak. I think this was the moment the war really ended for me. It was the strangest feeling. He seemed like an old very deep friend.'

Keeble has the crazy idea that one day he and Benitez will be able to visit the Falkland Islands together. As he told Benitez, 'After all, now we are both on the same side'.

From war to peace, this is also bedrock truth for farmers whose solidarity as colleagues will perhaps always outweigh the element of competition. It is not to deny the need for increasing efficiency, but an examination of the farming record will not find it wanting in this respect. I am not a proponent of dairy quotas as anything other than a stopgap solution, but it has to be said that the supposition that quotas mark an end to technical progress is more of an ideological conviction than an objective reality. Much thought and experience has now gone into the comparative costs of different strategies in production: whether more milk can be produced from forage, whether high yields or more cows is the road to follow, and how far pushing for maximum production is truly cost-effective. In brief, one had to study the most effective way of producing a certain quantity of milk without resort to continuous economies of scale. It is perfectly possible to argue that this might well be desirable for a time, and it certainly does not entirely eliminate the element of competition, as commonly equated with the spur to do better.

Progress can become too easily identified with economic imperatives and technical excellence that are measured in the profits generated. But is technical excellence reflected in our ability, as someone put it, to 'knock hell out of the competition', or to see such excellence spread throughout our industry? Manufacturing industry has tended to make the running in industrial philosophy, but farmers have a more complex cycle to master, and perhaps new elements to contribute. Both set out to meet a need but, in an age of consumerism, the refinements of equipment and the growth of sheer gadgetry go far beyond any reasonable definition of need. Instead, we set our standard by what the customer wants, while we deploy a massive advertising industry to make sure that his wants are stimulated in the desired direction.

Materialism has been called the mother of all the isms, and it certainly remains the most fertile source of ideas which divert us from long-term goals. Practices which have become built into the system are accepted as inevitable but, in an age of accelerating changes, there should be none that are beyond examination. A crop like tobacco may be a case in point, particularly if its cultivation depends on subsidies. The overwhelming evidence on lung cancer has led to falling sales in the West. The right of those who wish to continue smoking in the light of this can be defended. What cannot be defended is the campaign to increase the smoking of tobacco in Asia and Africa by promotions of dubious honesty which also draw young people into the habit. Farmers involved in tobacco growing would be well advised to look for alternative crops, while the question has to be asked whether the moral basis of the market economy is equal to this sort of challenge, or whether change only happens under government pressure.

Whatever our answer to that, changes are certain, and in an interdependent world, the nature of competition may be one field for change. Even now it is dawning on the Department of the Environment that the multiplication of new supermarkets on green field sites may not be an unmitigated blessing. At the same time, new ways of introducing the public to help-yourself bulk buying start to raise protests from the supermarket directors themselves. The 'king of the castle' approach may have had its day, and in a competitive world farmers may find that their solidarity worldwide has more to offer in cash terms than continuing to play the market, which sooner or later is bound to be loaded against them. Only then can economics become our servant and not our master.

What is more, such questions must be answered in the context of vital world issues and increasing doubts about what is truly in the national interest. World War Two mobilised people in a common purpose which was exceedingly powerful. Lesser wars, however, are triggered by lesser purposes, and may not command the allegiance of the whole nation. Trade wars are threatened for even more dubious reasons. Bilateral disputes, such as that between the US and Japan, become acute when one side is desperate to force a change, but the way ahead might become clearer in a multilateral context.

For Britain in Europe, trade issues are clearly a spur to involvement with the European Union, and arguments turn more on our independence among colleagues in the name of national sovereignty. This should be questioned: cooperation depends on trust, and if trust breaks down, common institutions are soon in trouble. It poses the question: are we committed to making these institutions work, or more concerned with our world position, however this may be defined? A separate view of economic life is becoming extremely difficult to sustain with any sense of reality. National boundaries may sustain and defend a particular way of life, but can hardly manage an independent economy. The cry that we will cooperate if it's in our national interest rings more than a little hollow.

Farmers are perhaps more aware of this than many. When it comes to feeding a hungry world with a rising population, the challenge must be to attempt it together. Europe and North America can bring a great deal of experience and potential to this, but it is not a purely technical matter. Reconciliation between rival forces involves new relationships, and has received a great boost from the marvellous change of direction achieved in South Africa. Professor Washington Okumu played a key role in the negotiations which helped Inkatha to participate in the South African elections at the very last moment. He is particularly aware of the need to understand what is in peoples' hearts. In a foreword to a recent book (*Witness For Ever*, by Michael Cassidy) which describes some of these encounters, he gives an interesting assessment.

There is a prevailing view in the West that tends to emphasise economic and materialistic dimensions of life at the expense of the spiritual. The adherents of this world view have accommodated to their detriment an intolerance to that which is spiritual. The co-existence of secular Western thought and sacred religious fervour as influences in the corridors of power in Western capitals is often characterised by an uneasy truce, which in times of crisis degenerates into a contempt for the spiritual. This may be germane to the lapses that have become an integral part of the articulation, implementation and overall comprehension of Western foreign policy, especially in its relations with Third World nations.

In many Third World, and particularly African, societies, the spiritual dimension of life forms an integral part of the 'whole', and is incomprehensible when fragmented from it – that is, if the 'whole' in some of these societies has not yet been deliberately compartmentalised to suit the conveniences of technological advancement, industrialisation and modernisation which characterise many Western societies. The deeply spiritual psyches of many Third World peoples make them more amenable to accepting from and attributing extraordinary occurrences to the divine. One hopes that the Third World peoples will not only retain this quality, but will in time help the more industrial and technologically advanced Western societies to regain it.

It is a judgement which is worthy of our reflection, and may be particularly relevant to the way we look at economic competition. In so far as we have influenced African countries, we may even have done a disservice in this respect. It may not be too late for us to be influenced in our turn.

Chapter 13
The Economics of Food Production

If capitalism is seen as an acceptance of the Western way, the suggestion that the West has won the 'cold war' is one more reflection on the limitations of conventional thinking. As on too many previous occasions, if we have won the war we are once more in danger of losing the peace. Those who are looking for the creation of wealth through capitalism, and for sharing on the road to democracy are at once confronted with the shortcomings of our Western models. Some expert advisers are even reduced to the formula, 'Do as we say, not as we do'.

This basically arises from the fact that Marx's reactions to capitalism led him to identify economic and political power as the only key to the forces of history. His reaction to the harsh inequalities of the industrial revolution became enshrined in the equally harsh extreme of communism. It was a misreading of the fundamental laws of economics, which Schumacher tried to redress in *Small is Beautiful*. The fact is that economics should be a tool for the management of money and of national budgets. It should not seek to lay down laws that are held to have an authority over human life commensurate with that of the Ten Commandments. Dr John Wibberley, formerly Head of Agriculture at the Royal Agricultural College, suggests that 'Economics is a social science for the service of mankind, rather than an inexorable physical force to which man has to be enslaved. While favouring maximum freedom for private enterprise profits by responsible means – with both bureaucracy and government intervention minimised – one cannot pretend there is anything near a free market in food and agricultural products.'

Not only is there no free market but, for all the cuts in subsidies, we are not about to achieve one in the next generation. The old joke about no two economists agreeing on how to tackle a particular scenario could in fact be taken as the sign of a healthy situation. This is not to say that there are no mathematical laws in economics, but rather that we should set out aims in terms of the needs of mankind before seeking how to fulfil them. Full employment is not something that is no longer attainable, it is more a question of how badly we want it. There is certainly no immutable law that the directors of big businesses will not give their best unless they have a six or seven figure salary. Nor that the volume of manufactured goods must increase constantly to satisfy some law of wealth creation. Henry Ford was pioneering when he installed the first assembly line to fulfil a vision of mass production. His vision was a car for every family. Lines computerised with robots represent technical progress, but it has to be asked, 'progress to where?'

Even in agriculture, this dilemma is acutely reflected in farms that are for ever growing, while the number of people employed shrinks. As one Canadian farmer remarked, 'you can either extend your land to the far horizon or you can have neighbours. But you can't have both.' He spoke as one who had actually reduced his area by 200ha. So there is no rock-solid reason why this trend should be regarded as inevitable, if we really want to change direction radically.

Meanwhile, in the other half of the globe, agriculture's strength is still unchallenged. The sheer weight of peasant farming numbers and the need for adequate nutrition keep it at the top of the agenda. Here, the tendency to urge on mechanisation has been curbed by the need to keep people employed and, if water is available for irrigation, the intensive nature of tropical production. As noted earlier, a farmer in the Eastern Cape (South Africa) declared that, against the advice of economists, he felt that he should employ as much labour on the farm as it could possibly carry. Who is to say that he was wrong, in face of South Africa's needs, especially when he was also pioneering in farm rural education?

In China, the great surge in food production which has followed the 'Household Contracted Responsibility System' has now spread into industry. Production in the rural industrial sector is now 50% of China's total industrial production. Yet the rush to industrialise is already creating fears for the future of food production. It is possible that it will be the farming millions who are the spearhead of a new thinking about agriculture, because they have yet to find their voice. For them, education may be more important than money in terms of social priorities. Several African leaders have voiced the thought that they have been educated more to make a career, and to gain riches and influence than to lead their countries. General Joseph Lagu, a leader from the southern Sudan, has said that Africa's elite have been educated for power rather than for the service of their people, while the unspoken thought is left that their access to higher education has been primarily in the West, and reflects the increasing materialism to be found there.

Certainly those who come out of agricultural colleges and settle on the land are the key to the future. Their role will be more crucial even than that of the research scientists and agri-business executives because the basics have to be in place before the accompaniments can bloom. So far, the vision for them has not extended beyond the hope that a modest prosperity and profitability can together provide the engine power for the nation's progress. Looking at largely illiterate peasants struggling to make a living can easily engender the thought that all that is required is their survival, while the more sophisticated construct a modern society. But those who really want to understand democracy come up against the truth that it stands or falls by the destiny and development of the individual. What is more, its continuance depends entirely on the values those individuals seek in their daily lives. Agriculture has a continuing and not diminishing role in the future of civilisation, and the guarantee of that may be embodied in the millions who now work on the land. Of course they are not destined to stay as they are, but neither should they be simply the object of government planning. Now is the time for them to take their destiny into their own hands, not in some proletarian revolution but in a fresh awakening to what farmers have to give in a world that has lost its way.

It is almost as though we had to start again from the beginning.

The manager of a 1,200 acre arable and dairy farm in the UK who accepts the logic of larger units as inevitable, told me he thought of leaving in a few years to do something else before retirement loomed. He gave as one of his reasons the stress of the job on a man approaching fifty, and the feeling that there might be more creative work to be done in the developing world. A year later he had been made redundant under a policy, which is becoming increasingly prevalent, of grouping even large farms under a single manager, with the hands-on management left to a working foreman. Perhaps that is the logic of capitalism's own brand of collective farming, but should the judgement be left only to the accountant?

In the light of this, I was fascinated to discover William Keegan's thesis in his book, *The Spectre of Capitalism*. He puts forward the proposition that capitalism is 'not a system, not an ideology, but a way of life'. Could this open the road to liberation? For farming is also a way of life in which the main function of economics is to secure a livelihood and the means to raise a family. The old joke about the farmer who won the Pools and told the usual enquirers that this would not change his lifestyle but simply allow him to go on farming, makes the point. Farming may often swallow up capital, but it brings satisfactions that are not lightly to be put aside. Such thoughts, of course, tend to be heretical to the ethos of our times, which demands that the first test must be profitability: not just viability, but ever-increasing margins to represent return on capital.

It is striking, when looking at forecasts made after the final conclusion of GATT's Uruguay Round, that the only major disadvantaged area is Africa. In the estimates published by the OECD, Africa is forecast to be worse off by rather over £2 billion, while Europe is the largest gainer with rather over £60 billion. Those figures alone might suggest that there is something wrong with the terms of trade with Africa. They certainly suggest that Europe's wider responsibilities are called in question if such a scenario is simply left to take its course. GATT has now been superseded by a World Trade Organisation which will regulate its functions and adjudicate on disputes. It is to be hoped that its agricultural arm will not accept the definition of itself which has prevailed to date, and that the need to include environmental considerations will result in major change. A one way street to trade liberalisation is not a sufficient answer to the worldwide disparities which exist today. In this situation, of course, Africa's farming should be its trump card. For a country to feed itself may not result in an impressive GNP, but it removes the need for imports of staple foods. It could also remove the forecast £2 billion disadvantage.

Keegan suggests that economics and politics have a symbiotic relationship. So, if people's lives are left to the vagaries of the free market, capitalism is indeed a dangerous spectre. There must be an interaction of markets and government, and it is that which has been accepted in agriculture, even if trying to get it right can become an excessively complicated business. Moves towards simplification must be welcomed without accepting that the widely quoted example of New Zealand is likely to be valid worldwide. What is needed is for Europeans to play the same game under the same rules, not to have a unified approach on the style in which the game should be played. Nor should the rules include the enforcement of free trade worldwide, when the disparities of opportunity involved are so great.

A New Zealander on the staff of the World Trade Organisation told me he felt that opening access to new markets could be as significant as ending export subsidies. He instanced Japan, which opened its market to butter, but levied a 500% tariff. One immediate result was that the French restaurants in Japan started to import French butter. Their customers were looking to experience everything French, and were quite prepared to pay for the privilege. This is an interesting sidelight on how affluent societies work, but it is hardly relevant to those in real need of food.

So the thought of simplifying the approach should also remind us that agricultural trade is only the tip of the iceberg. The bulk of food produced is traded within the country that produces it, and it is for that reason that a degree of protection remains a live issue. A paper such as *The Economist*, founded to celebrate the repeal of the Corn Laws, may go so far as to suggest that trade need no longer make any concessions to geography, but that has nothing to do with the realities of farming or even the environmental cost of transport. A country's sense of its national identity rests in its land. Its soil is literally the rock from which it is hewn, and its physical guarantee for the future. The arguments about security in case of war may be receding, but those of survival in face of economic hardship remain as compelling as ever. Successful subsistence continues to be a more fundamental issue than the wealth, whether real or imaginary, displayed in the financial columns by large companies. The failure to accord agriculture its primary place in matters of development has now long been recognised, at least in principle. Yet there still seems to be a failure to understand that cheap food has always been the enemy of agricultural development. Britain's cheap food policy between the world wars ensured the neglect of her agriculture. Countries whose agriculture is more vulnerable have been threatened with division between plantation crops that earn much needed currency, and subsistence farming which keeps the nation fed. Both are important elements in the full economic picture, but the achievement in export earnings has often been bought at the expense of the long battle by the plantation workers for a living wage.

Moreover, in face of the complications of subsidised production, economists today are unable to say what the true world price of grain would be without them. The only way to find out is for rich countries to cease subsidising their exports. It should be a priority aim, because subsidies are a major factor in holding prices down. Prices would rise, and we are all interested to know by how much. Whatever the final outcome, farmers in the North would find a genuine basis for solidarity with farmers in the South based on actual costs. It would not eliminate the role of government, but it would certainly restore some feeling of sense and simplicity.

It is interesting that Thailand, one of the few countries successfully to avoid the fate of colonisation, has small farmers who to some extent share in her destiny as a food exporter. To a degree, they have a foot in both camps, yet they remain under considerable economic threat, more for reasons of marketing than production. Although Thailand was a member of the Cairns Group pushing for freer trade in agriculture, there were at the same time, as a Bangkok journalist pointed out, calls for the Government to put more money into agriculture. This may not be as contradictory as it might appear, because investment in agriculture could bring quick returns and enhance its already competitive position. Indeed this is evident at Sakon Nakhon, in the north east of Thailand, where foreign companies have organised the growing of tomatoes for export. This is a diversification of their programme pioneered by Dr Jameson Bell, an American plant breeder who has spent a lifetime in Asia, and still returns to Thailand in his eighties. He is an outstanding example of that rare breed, who have a lot of patience and a listening ear. What is more, he believes livestock to be an essential component of good crop husbandry which maintains soil fertility. Organic manures are frequently referred to locally as 'Bell's Gold'.

At Lam Nam Oon, the irrigation project which I visited, there is capacity to serve 75,000 acres. Traditional crops, like rice, are handled by local merchants, but nine companies share the recent development of fruit and vegetables, where Bell has supervised the introduction of hybrid tomatoes and the training of farmers in their culture. He points out, by way of illustration, that rice growing involves three major management decisions and tomato growing forty seven. But the success of the local growers is attested by yields of 10 tons per rai (just under half an acre) and by the fact that a company effort to grow a crop on its own land with hired labour could not match this performance.

At the time of my visit, Bell was conducting trials on varieties of sorghum to grow for green fodder for cattle, and training farmers on seed-rate, depth of planting and fertiliser placement. Khun Banchong, the head of the Lam Nam Oon development at that time, is something of a hero from the days when government officers were ready targets for the communists or other dissidents. He considered cattle essential for fertility on what is basically a poor sandy soil, and felt people were beginning to appreciate that one really good beast could be more profitable than several scrags. He had also introduced a baler for rice straw, manufactured to his own design at a fraction of the cost of importing, in order to start using the thousands of tons of straw burnt unnecessarily. Shades of the UK a few years back!

At Lam Nam Oon (LNO) the original aim was simply to get rice farmers to grow tomatoes for canning in the dry season. In the first year, 100 farmers signed up to grow tomatoes, but only 27 actually did so. A wider vision was clearly needed by the three main groups involved, the farmers, the companies and the Government. This led to the creation of the LNO Production and Marketing Programme as a vehicle for cooperation. The farmers provided the land, labour and capital for production. The companies provided the market, the supply of inputs, the technology, the transport and the economics of both production and marketing. The Government, in this case the Irrigation Department, provided the infrastructure. They changed their old ways of closing down the water delivery system without regard to crop requirements and timing, and began scheduling canal repairs at times when water was not needed by crops.

In the space of 10 years, 6000 farmers and 2000 migrant workers have become involved. Four factories are in operation for tomato processing, and six international seed companies are producing a wide variety of vegetable seeds for world distribution. Farmers' meetings have brought social needs to the fore, with the result that two schools, a health clinic and a library have been established. A more balanced development is thus taking place overall, though of course it is still in its infancy.

What can be marked up to the achievement so far is the commitment of the companies, through their staff, to helping the farmers in every detail of their production. They are on the spot when needed at weekends, and concerned to establish profitability. They contract to take all produce at negotiated prices, while the

Government may have a role as referee in cases of dispute. Already farm costs have been substantially reduced by good production and efficient marketing, but effective farmers' organisations have still to be developed. They will be needed not only to give better balance to the partnership triangle, but to contribute to the growing need for an overall view of rural development in a rapidly expanding economy.

For while many of the immediate developments benefit the farmers substantially, there remains a question mark over the longer term. The rampant goldrush in available markets may yet prove a threat to the farmers' way of life, simply because any political salvation seems to be lacking. At Lam Nam Oon, I heard the current Prime Minister dubbed 'an eel on rollerskates', a description which rather took my fancy. But it was clear that it referred to his capacity as a sharp operator, rather than any expectations that he was heading for a fall. Politicians may come and go but corruption continues. So the struggle for a new motivation may be the only way forward. The King's Agricultural Projects have made an important contribution in this direction, as has the dedicated work of a section of the Royal Thai Army. That is where the farmers' opportunity lies, if they can establish new standards among themselves, and give them credibility in the wider world. Certainly that is the understanding of some of those coming out of agricultural colleges and universities, particularly if they have any desire to farm themselves. They could and should be the backbone of the future, as suggested in an earlier chapter.

Meanwhile, the economics of subsistence tend to be ignored because such a large part of them lies outside the realm of monetary practice and theory. Yet in terms of human numbers, and certainly of human need, their importance could even now be the greater. Such importance is inevitably measured more in human than in monetary terms: certainly the value of the food grown will be unlikely to figure in calculations of Gross National Product. Equally certainly, new horizons open as such farmers leave the strictly subsistence for the cash economy.

It is striking to watch such a transformation taking place, as in the Anand pattern dairy cooperatives in India described in Chapter 15. The farmer with a single buffalo who brings even a jug of milk to the village depot receives payment in cash perhaps for the first time in his or her life. That money marks an entry into what has become known as the consumer society. We are all consumers, but the farming industry is the only one which numbers the whole of humanity among its customers. Sophisticated consumers have come to believe that the smaller the proportion of their income they spend on necessities, the more will be available for luxury and leisure to back the unspoken theory that this equates with a satisfying life. Yet it should be clear to the most casual observer that there is no obvious correlation between income and satisfaction.

That being so, the thought arises that paying more for our food might after all make economic sense. Added value in food processing has raised the cost of food mainly by packaging and through convenience foods which save time in preparation and cooking. Real prices of food have consistently fallen in response to improving productivity, but the current controversy over farm subsidies and their cost to the taxpayer may yet produce some surprising results. Few critics pause to consider the differences between food production and manufacturing industry. The latter sets its price on the basis of cost of production plus a margin for profit. When sales falter it reduces production and dismisses workers. The farmer, on the other hand, finds the quantity of his production is decided by the season, and that the price rarely bears direct relation to the cost of production. If there is surplus, land cannot be set aside without cost, nor can workers be dismissed without dislocating the whole system. In most commodities, moreover, long-term storage is not only expensive but involves serious loss of value as well.

To equate low costs and maximum profit with efficiency is no doubt the essence of good accountancy. It is certainly what the money markets are looking for. But the success of Japanese industry has been attributed, among other things, to management's conviction that the workers may be more important than the shareholders or perhaps, more accurately, that the long-term benefit of the shareholders will be best guaranteed by this assumption. Because if efficiency becomes disconnected from production and satisfying human needs, it is a purely paper concept bolstered more by figures than the reality on the ground.

It is important to remember this lesson in contemplating the depletion of rural populations, especially if the resulting increase in the cities is almost wholly negative. For it must be, if there is no work to be found there either.

No less an authority than J M Keynes has said that we should not 'overestimate the importance of the economic problem, or sacrifice to its supposed necessities other matters of greater and more permanent significance'. This is an important rider, and warns us against repeating the heresy that capitalism is in some way an ideology with its own sacred dogma. It puts the needs of man in body, mind and spirit firmly back at the top of the agenda.

William Keegan suggests that, with growing threats from environmental and irrigation problems, capitalism may indeed have to start planning its future at just the moment when the collapse of communism has made the concept of planning anathema. He points out that Japan operates a high degree of long-term planning in its industrial sector. Japanese capitalism could be called industrial capitalism which is 'administratively guided'. In contrast US capitalism is rather consumer directed. But the wilder excesses of the capitalist way have been curbed to some extent by the democratic process. In the United States, under President Johnson, there was a 50% increase in welfare spending in pursuit of what he labelled the 'Great Society'. Today, public spending is being cut back, though mainly on the prescription that privatisation can do the necessary work more efficiently. Yet extreme swings of the pendulum are not so much self-correcting as an indication of the need for fresh motivation. Meanwhile, on the other side of the divide, Khruschev's 1961 boast about producing more industrial goods than the US was made good by 1986. Yet all it heralded was the abrupt end of the Soviet Empire.

By the same token, it was vital in the reunification of Germany that capital should flow east, rather than that labour should flow west. Much has been made of the strain which this put on the West German economy, but it is now becoming apparent that considerable achievements have been registered in a comparatively short space of time, not least in the sector of arable farming. But what economics has not been able to do is to heal the wounded spirit.

Ricardo Semler, the Brazilian industrialist, quotes Henry Ford as saying, 'A great business is really too big to be human'. Semler suggests that much about growth is really about ego and greed rather than business strategy. He finds growth through acquisition exciting, glamorous and ulcer-inducing. He says that 'at Semco we have consciously decided to stop growing'. 'Yet', he adds, 'today we are still expanding (1993) and expecting to sign an agreement with one hundred and fifty engineering associates in the coming months. But most of these won't be employees, they'll be partners. Similarly, we will grow our sales force through our new network of satellite companies, consultants and partnerships.'

All of this may seem to be straying from the economics of food production. But Keegan poses the question, is it possible for every country, or even the majority of developing countries to 'catch up' with the developed? It is clearly a question which cannot be answered off the cuff but, for me, it raises for me again the position of agriculture as the starting point. If we can get things right there, is it too much to hope that we may find ourselves on the path to longer- term solutions?

Mr Renato Ruggiero, the Director General of the World Trade Organisation, has made a point of proclaiming that Africa's trade is the top priority on the international agenda. If we can stick to that point, it may prove the acid test of real progress, but the starting point is to have faith in what farming can deliver.

Chapter 14
The Food Chain

I had intended to leave my excursion into economics at the level of food production, since that is the end which principally concerns the farmer. But the constant exhortations for farmers to look to their marketing make it necessary to go further. That decision has also been inspired by reading a book called *The Food System – a Guide*, by Geoff Tansey and Tony Worsley. It has a wealth of information, excellently set out, and a great many will find its subject a fruitful field on which to ponder. It provides a real stimulus to thought.

In a paragraph of the chapter on 'The Changing Balance of Power' between processors, distributors and caterers, Tansey and Worsley underline how fluid the present situation actually is.

> Retailers themselves might find their role changing, however, with the use of interactive technology now becoming available in the store and the home. All this will influence retail formats and location, and will offer the opportunities for competition from new sources – directly from manufacturers or from communication industries. This may raise the question of who is the middle man. If interactive technology is added to the above trends, then radically different food retailing patterns could emerge, with consumers interacting with people right down the food chain. Indeed, the whole idea of a linear food chain is being discarded as interaction increases across different parts of it. Whatever happens, there is a fascinating battle going on for who processes – in the factory, home or small business – the food that goes into people's stomachs worldwide.

For the moment, however, we have to live with the situation as it is. The farmer is acutely aware that his share of the total cash value of food is steadily diminishing. In the United States in 1991, on-farm value of food represented 22% of the total (*Food Review*, Vol. 12 No 2). In the UK, even in the late 1980s, it was already as low as 15% while, also in 1991, Nestlé spent 28% of its total turnover on raw materials.

So only major shifts in farm gate prices will have much impact on the price to the consumer. In these circumstances, 'adding value' has become the recommended way towards improving the farmer's income. Certainly, it makes sense for poorer countries to develop food processing industries, which not only generate cash and employment, but also reduce needless transport.

Branded products then become the way to try and catch the consumer's eye, but even well-known brands need to be assessed for real value. Nabisco Brands Inc., for example, describes developments in its 'Planters' product peanuts which show that such moves are mainly aimed at keeping the brand alive and fresh in the public's perception.

Nabisco's Senior Vice President said this in a speech in 1983 (Food Manufacturers Federation, London).

> You can buy shelled peanuts for, I think, about 25c per pound, and we sell our peanuts under 'Planters' brand for about $3 per pound... The results of all this activity (on new products) have been first of all to maintain a brand alive and interesting. Perhaps more importantly, every one of those extensions had a better gross margin than the original product.
>
> What does that allow us to do? Firstly, it allows us to advertise, and spend a great deal of money keeping our franchise and brands strong. It allows us to put money into promotion and to make a better contribution to our profitability, which is what it is all about.

Clearly this means that food policy should concern farmers a great deal more than it has, because the share of total food value going to the producer is constantly being squeezed. Financial muscle and the control of raw materials largely determines who gets what benefits from food, so it is important that the farmer does his homework, and understands the context in which he has to fight his corner.

The main challenge does not lie in taking over other people's territory, but rather in winning recognition as a valid partner in shaping the total operation. Some may see this as participating in comprehensive vertical integration from the plough to the plate such as has been embodied in organisations like Cargill. The majority would probably prefer some form of producer cooperation, which allows a degree of independence to be combined with a more creative approach to farming's potential contribution to the picture as a whole. This mainly involves us in becoming stronger and better-organised sellers.

Many co-operative groups have addressed themselves to the task with varying success. The British do not seem to be natural cooperators and, for the most part, have lagged behind their colleagues in Europe. Most successful initiatives have started in quite a small way with a core of committed enthusiasts who are prepared to do the basic spadework usually required, and normally unpaid.

Meadow Valley Livestock, to which we belong, is a co-operative group for the marketing of livestock to the meat trade on a dead-weight basis. Historically, it had a slow start. For some years it was a small group of committed farmers, who were sustained by faith in their goal more than any benefits they could offer potential members. But the logic of current developments has worked a transformation and now it is a growing force in the market, selling, in 1995, 2700 lambs, 5900 pigs and 550 cattle each week.

With 400 A, or fully committed, members, and 2000 B, it is now well placed to participate in building new relationships within the meat trade. Premiums for quality may not yet be all they might but, with a fair number of abattoirs going bankrupt, the group can cover from its insurance fund any members who might have been caught in that particular trap if selling individually. Contacts can also extend beyond the abattoirs to the supermarkets and butchers. This brings farmers first hand information on the requirements of the market, and the chance to aim at the type and quality of animal which corresponds to identified outlets in the region, whether for local consumption or export. Farmers may be latecomers to modern marketing, but it is certainly not too late for them to play a major role.

Indeed, the growth of farm shops, while labelled a diversification, could more properly be called an extension of existing business. They have an exceptional opportunity to provide value for money, if they have easy access and are attractive to visit. They may not be an easy option in terms of planning and operation, but they can certainly help a farmer to add value to what he has produced.

Meanwhile, eating out has become a hallmark of affluent societies. In the US in 1990, almost half of the food dollars spent went on meals and snacks away from home; in the UK the figure was about a third of total spending. So caterers have become the section of the food industry providing most employment, and the fast food industry has been particularly successful in this expansion.

McDonalds had grown from a single hamburger restaurant in 1954, to over 13,000 outlets in 63 countries by 1992. It plans to keep growing but, while 84% of its restaurants in the US are owned and run by franchisees, only 11% are in this category in the UK. This might suggest that, while the formula is proving immensely successful round the globe, it may not become universally indigenous.

In a parallel way, street foods (ready to eat foods and drinks prepared and/or sold by vendors in the streets) are also a vast global business. 'It is a multi-billion dollar activity which boasts no multinational corporations, yet provides a livelihood for millions, and food for hundreds of millions, especially the poor' (FAO, 1992). It is not an activity which has been officially encouraged but, despite the difficulties and poor hygiene, serious incidents of food poisoning seem comparatively rare. An amazing variety of foods are offered, and the poor, crowding into growing cities, would certainly be worse off without them.

As Tansey and Worsley point out, the consumers of the affluent world are offered an abundance of foods to buy, ever more conveniently presented but less and less under their control. Meanwhile, hunger and malnutrition persist among the poor, and Tansey and Worsley cite the largest food aid programme in the world as being the US Government's effort for its own poor, totalling $29 billion in 1991. Lest we in Britain are tempted to point the finger at such a revelation, it is as well to remember that Oxfam has recently decided to use a small part of its budget to alleviate poverty at home rather than overseas. Though we may welcome such an initiative, it is a shaming commentary on the way things have been going here.

Tansey and Worsley's general approach to the future and the changes which are in full flood, is to say that new alliances are possible between the interests involved.

> Power may be compared, politely, to a dung heap. In a heap, dung stinks, does no good and may pollute. But spread out and scattered over the fields, it fertilises and life can blossom. Power is like dung. The skills, knowledge and technology that we need to have power over our food, must be spread for an effective system. The key challenge is to transform the institutions and design the tools so that power is shared and spread.'

This is another clear call for democratic development, and a question-mark over the concentration of commercial activity in ever larger concerns.

It has, perhaps, become too easily overlooked that shedding jobs in the cause of efficiency also leads to a reduction in competition. Take-overs and amalgamations, with resultant job losses, are in the news daily. They are accepted as the logic of the market without any need to prove their economic worth. Yet clearly the market changes as this process continues. The giants may still be in competition with one another, but a vested interest is created in their continued existence. Indeed, many of them have budgets on a par with the budgets of the smaller nations, so that any symbiotic relationship with government becomes hopelessly unbalanced. The mega-companies may declare their independence from politics in order to concentrate on business development, but the realities on the ground rapidly undermine the credibility of this exercise.

It is even possible that some companies inhibit rather than stimulate the development needed in situations of poverty. They may be multinational, but they prove unable to adapt their operation to the needs of individual countries. It is assumed that only one way of working is required worldwide. That all should aspire to follow the dictates of orthodox economies rather than explore fresh ways of doing business.

This can only result in a pressure to conform, and the tendency for the most successful trainees to be those who accept the way things have been achieved up to date, rather than those who look for a seriously different future. This is not to say that changes will not still happen, or that new technology will not be embraced as fast as it offers greater efficiency. But it will not encourage those who, in current parlance, would like to try to 'think the unthinkable.' Such nonconformists could be a danger to share prices, and there are few with the strength of mind to ignore fluctuations in the money markets.

Such questions link with the current situation in the development of scientific research, which has begun to move from government to private finance. Recent figures apparently suggest that about 60% of agricultural research in the US and the UK is now privately funded. Not more that 10% of such research is privately financed in the less-developed countries, with most of that being concentrated in larger countries such as Brazil, Mexico, Argentina and India.

There is a conflict of principle here which needs to be addressed, because only government-financed research is publicly shared.

Generally speaking, governments aim at increasing basic knowledge, developing farming techniques and improving the welfare of society. In the UK, we have benefited enormously from the sharing of knowledge promoted by ADAS (Agricultural Development and Advisory Service) and other previously public bodies.

Privately-financed research, on the other hand, is used by companies to develop new products and seize a competitive advantage in technology. It is contended that only large companies can find the money needed to finance research, and that this confirms the importance of patent laws which allow them to recoup their outlay. It is frequently quoted that 'he who pays the piper, calls the tune,' but, of course, it also follows that the number of tunes may be restricted. Perhaps scientists could have a greater share in innovation, something which involves being concerned with product strategy as well as product development. They should not be limited to pursuing a commercial brief already defined and laid down.

Academics and all those who wish to pursue knowledge for its own sake need a source of finance which leaves them free to make their own decisions, whether it comes from government or university endowments. Even in China, professors are complaining that the money involved in high-speed industrialisation is creaming off the talent needed to maintain high standards in the universities. So there are twin issues at stake: both the financing of research programmes and the mobilisation of bright young people to pursue them.

Here in Britain, the trend to less spending on fundamental research in favour of more privately funded 'near market' research, is now being widely criticised. Perhaps the realisation that we are already moving from surplus to scarcity will prompt some second thoughts. In any event, the real need is for some sort of strategy for the future which is fully shared with the general public. There are too many issues of grave public concern to settle for anything less. A balance needs to be struck on issues of agricultural development, full employment and public health and nutrition. It will not come from the market, but only from the joint counsels of all those involved, in the light of people's needs.

The scare about BSE in cattle is only the latest in a long line of controversies which have come under the spotlight and then sunk from public consciousness. In this case our veterinary delegates to Brussels have been adamant that the precautions taken are all that were required, and that further slaughter is unnecessary. Nevertheless, they have been embarrassed on Britain's behalf by the revelation that the regulations at abattoirs have been seriously breached, and by the cost-cutting approach of the British Government, which decreed that qualified 'vets' were not required to oversee livestock for slaughter, despite their acceptance by other countries. It also appears that a report on the UK's strategy for eliminating BSE was called for in 1994, but no documentation was offered, a serious neglect of necessary teamwork with European colleagues.

From the farmers' angle, a recent defence for not labelling the ingredients of animal feeding stuffs encapsulates the problem of the customer. The spokesman for a major feed manufacturer gave two reasons for not labelling – one, that a feed might contain a novel ingredient which gave them the edge on the competition; two, that some farmers might not understand the issues involved in including a particular ingredient. This has been the accepted commercial logic but one which is rapidly becoming outdated. Viewed from the climate of opinion into which we are moving, both observations would be powerful arguments for disclosure.

This, of course, is equally true for the consumer and the public at large. Perhaps the next step is to take a more positive interest in our food all the time, rather than only when a problem is raised. Although labelling is improving, a surprisingly large number of people never read labels, and continue to have illusions about what they are buying. A leading brand of chicken stock cube apparently contains beef bones as its major ingredient (it also contains less chicken than salt). In a more familiar field perhaps, fish fingers are not required to reach any particular level of fish content, but they must declare on their labels how much they do contain. Not unexpectedly, there is a wide variation between brands, and those who seek the cheapest may simply be buying less fish. So it is perhaps surprising that the popularity of cookery books and the rise in eating out in restaurants have not raised the level of awareness on these questions.

The so called 'street foods' may be at a disadvantage in terms of hygiene, but they are not lacking in terms of taste and variety. Asia particularly has a rich array of spices. Although the popularity of Indian and Chinese restaurants is not touched on in the next chapter, it is as well to remember, even in the face of hunger and malnutrition, that those countries have a valued tradition in food handling and preparation. Large parts of the Asian food system may lie outside western experience, but that system functions quite effectively nonetheless!

It is clearly premature to talk about a world food system with a settled pattern of development. Even so, it should be regarded as a matter of urgency for farmers to get more involved. They are an essential factor in the total equation, and cannot afford to be spectators from behind the farm gate. Mastering computer technology not only helps with digesting farm figures, but also offers access to important commercial information.

Chapter 15
Indian Farmers and Asian Possibilities

Some Western visitors find the poverty of India hard to take. They are unable to penetrate to the spirit of the people and, when their visit is over, they feel that they must hurry away. Others are fascinated, not least by the cheerfulness and resilience of many of the poorest. They have massive needs, but they also have something to give us. BBC correspondent Mark Tully is one of those who has given his heart to India, and whose reports are informed by sympathy and understanding. Countless others have been won on a much shorter acquaintance, and I count myself among these. In an age when nationalism seems to be rising in the world, it could be called a glimpse of the personality of a nation: a perception of people and their character conveyed through observation, conversations and friendships rather than cultural studies or statistical analysis. This is the genesis of a love affair with another nation, and study can duly deepen and enlarge it. It is then that apparently random observations come together to make up the inner picture we carry and which illustrates the character of a nation. For many, perhaps, it begins with the sheer mass of humanity; the crowded shanty towns, trains crammed with passengers and streets alive with mixed multitudes of people and vehicles. A kaleidoscope of activity which completely defies analysis, but gives a vivid image of city life.

For me, it then led on to the villages and the real heartland of India, the contrasts of arid brown and gorgeous green, relentless sun and life-giving water. This is the baptism of farming in tropical and semi-tropical climates. A stunning speed of growth, and then perhaps a sudden death until the ultimate rebirth after a long wait for rain. It may seem a different world, but nature operates under one law, and farmers the world over are one people. The experience of a few weeks can soon prove the point, and leave one less breathless under the multitude of new impressions.

Even an Indian sometimes feels a need to come to terms with his own country. Satya Banerji, a well-known and dedicated Trade Unionist in Calcutta, described to me how as a young man he set out on a bicycle to pedal round India and get to know his own countrymen. Two thousand miles later he was undoubtedly richer in experience and wiser in judgement. Such a deliberate expedition catches the imagination: a romantic journey, perhaps, but full of down-to-earth discoveries.

India is particularly fortunate to have had a world figure like Mahatma Gandhi to introduce her to a new generation of travellers. Not least to the British, for whose soul and conscience he never ceased to fight. It is remarkable that in a speech made in Madras in 1915, he could say, 'I discovered that the British Empire has certain ideals with which I have fallen in love, and one of those ideals is that every subject of the British Empire has the freest scope possible for his energy and honour, and whatever he thinks is due to his conscience. I think that is true of the British Government as it is true of no other government.' Four years later, of course, came Britain's horrific fall from grace in the Amritsar massacre. But while it may have tempered the Mahatma's judgement of the realities of British character, it did not dim his faith in God nor his belief that the failures in himself and those around him could be redeemed.

He felt the failure represented in India's partition so deeply that he was unable to join in the celebrations of independence. Yet he spent himself to the end in an effort to reach out to Muslim people, and stem the communal violence. In Bengal, he largely succeeded, but he paid with his life when misguided Hindu fundamentalists plotted his assassination. His was a questing spirit nurtured in the Hindu tradition but always ready to reach out to people of other faiths. A unique blend of humour and practicality illuminated his pursuit of ideas and his experiments in truth. As Dr Frank Buchman was moved to remark, 'To walk with Gandhi was like walking with Aristotle.'

It is no digression to dwell for a moment on the giant shadow cast by Gandhi, because his ideals, though not practised by the millions who still admire him today, remain a beacon light. There are certainly still many for whom that light remains a guide on the road. One such is my friend Arun Chavan, activator of the Verala Development Society, and our link with Indian farming when our local farmers' group in Herefordshire decided to look beyond the confines of Europe. A university professor of English with family land in the village of Pirathe Kavan, he had been invited by local farmers to help them at weekends, mainly because he knew the administrative procedures, and could make letters and telephone calls yield some result. As a boy, he had been brought up by an uncle who was a convinced communist and a militant atheist. While not sharing the atheism, Arun was much influenced by his uncle's passion for social justice, and the breaking down of caste barriers. It became a fundamental part of his belief in the need for a radical transformation of existing society. For that reason, perhaps, there came a moment when he resigned from his teaching post and devoted himself full-time, but without salary, to the cause of the farmers and rural development.

In many ways it was a commitment of his life to India's future and an expression of his faith in the peoples of India. Although, when I first met him some eight years later, and someone commented on the way God seemed to have guided a particular move, he could say, 'Coincidence perhaps?' and raise a quizzical eyebrow. Certainly, the Verala Society, which he has served so well, has had its setbacks as well as its successes. Yet it has stuck to the road, and in 1995 celebrated its jubilee of twenty five years with an expansion of staff, and an increasing recognition of its influence. Arun himself was given the John Dalvi Award by the Leslie Sawhny Programme of Training for Democracy, which cited his example of 'dedicated individual effort and outstanding teamwork'.

Based at Sangli in the south of Maharashtra, the Verala Development Society is run by an Executive Board of seven farmers and one full-time organiser in Arun. Starting with lift irrigation, it has also stimulated action on tree planting, sisal and grape cultivation, school and road building, and weaving and farming cooperatives. As the society's brochure states, 'The society was founded by a group of village activists. Keeping itself aloof from considerations of caste, and of the partisan passions of political strife, it has aimed at the development of rural communities.'

To those who ask how we have been able to help, I am forced to admit that we have certainly received more than we have given, although, where a true partnership can be forged, it is perhaps inappropriate to call for a balance sheet. Certainly it has been a precious and priceless education for all those from the group who have been able to travel to Sangli and meet some of those involved there. Not only has it been an opportunity to see a different sort of farming, but also a different approach. The perceptions of the Indian spirit in town and village lift a curtain on a different world, which is in most cases denied to the tourist. The legendary enterprise in unsocial hours and service of the Indian merchant, and his mechanical ingenuity with spent machinery, are seen on their home ground. Exported to Africa and the UK, they are an exotic product, but, at home, they are part of a national character which embodies a common approach to life and resilience in adversity, while simultaneously embracing an endless diversity. Already six of our group have been able to make the journey, while Arun himself has also visited us. So it has become more personal than simply participating in a distant project, however good the feedback of information. One moves from backing a good project to beginning to share a purpose for what a new relationship between Britain and India might offer.

On the other side of the balance sheet our most tangible contribution has been financial. We committed ourselves to a regular but modest annual contribution of £400, which helps to keep the wheels turning while projects are being prepared, as there are several charities which may support them once a plan has been quantified and costed. It is not always appreciated how much work and paper planning are needed to bring projects to the starting line, and it is a time when those involved still need the wherewithal to live. Occasionally, we bumped into needs almost by accident. The rattle of looms in the weaving shed is a serious assault on the ears, and the earplugs first tried had not been well received, and were ignored. With further enquiry we discovered an acceptable type, and found, much to our surprise, that they were manufactured quite close to us in the Midlands. More recently, there was a time when we had raised £250 to send Vasant Patil, Arun's right-hand-man, to Israel on an irrigation course. In the event, the course was cancelled, and Vasant enquired if the money could be put to a biogas plant at his family home in a neighbouring village, particularly for the benefit of the women folk. He and his family live in Sangli, but it was agreed that the extended family in the village should benefit, and a two cubic metre biogas plant was duly installed and connected with the toilet. At the last visit it was providing gas to cook with for a considerable party and the toilet was quite spotless. A small step in itself, it is likely to encourage others to follow suit.

But the long-term benefits are certainly to be found in the opportunity to watch the developments in a particular local situation. Sangli is a busy centre for farmers' marketing but, although the Krishna river provides some irrigation, much of the district is brown and barren under the constant threat of drought. I have only once seen the Verala river full of water, and that was on my first visit in 1978. But small dams or bunds in the dry watercourses and percolation tanks in natural basins have all helped to hold back what water there is, both for local irrigation and to maintain the underground water level. Otherwise, wells are always being deepened in a vain chase to reach down to a falling level. This is the most fundamental of the farmers' battles, and the fact that farming morale in 1993 was scarcely dented by a rainfall of only eight inches says much for the confidence which accompanies some evidence of progress.

Visible signs of this progress can be seen in cash crops such as dessert grapes and raisins, fruits such as jujube and pomegranate and, more controversially, sugar cane (controversial because sugar factories become centres of capital and cash, which may go to oil the wheels of political machines as much as to social objectives such as schools and hospitals). But the infrastructure is not neglected. The Verala Society has built both roads and schools, and is now embarking on building homes for the homeless, that is to say those who are camping out in hovels and who, for the most part, have to survive on casual labour.

The house-building programme was no sooner underway than an earthquake struck in the east of Maharashtra. So in January 1994 the Verala Society was able to offer to build 190 houses in two villages of the area, using the building design and training programme already in practice. Improvements have had to be made in the roofing against any future earthquake risk, but now the complete technology is in place for low-cost, do-it-yourself houses. In Sangli, these are financed by a small deposit and a fixed-rate loan. For the earthquake area, the capital will be put up half by Indian sources and half by the EZE (Protestant churches) charity in Germany. At the same time, Herefordshire Farmers have tripled their usual annual contribution to £1200 to assist this generous initiative and with the extra cost of having to work over 200kms from the Sangli base.

Within such a framework, social activities begin to develop, some more successful than others. The Verala Society has sponsored adult education for women, courses in dress-making with the use of sewing machines, youth club activities, environmental camps and more ambitious efforts in co-operation for the marketing of farm products, and for the manufacture of textiles through weaving. This last now includes factory space for around 250 looms and, though it may not be immensely profitable, it has remained viable. What is more, it has enabled men to stay with their families in their own villages, instead of having to go to Bombay, where they would be housed in crowded dormitories.

Behind all these developments, of course, are people, and part of the value in building personal links is the chance to see the emergence of some outstanding characters. Vasant is the Verala Society's chief operator in the field, a practical man who can train others from a confidence in his own skills. It is a joy to take a meal with his wife and children, because the home is so peaceful and orderly. One can only describe him as well organised. P S Thakur, a retired government servant, provides the technical experience to support the farm programmes. He is a Brahmin who doesn't mind getting his hands dirty, and has wisdom acquired from experience. Dilip Savashe is a young farmer who is wholehearted both in his farming and his support for the society. His father, still active, is one of the veteran 'freedom fighters' whose service has been recognised with a state pension. Ram Yadav, the President of the Weaving Co-operative, is a man whose faithfulness has held the enterprise together through plenty of difficulties. He is one who has a listening ear and gives thought to what people tell him.

Further afield from the society's immediate orbit are others who work in a similar spirit and are part of the pattern of renewal which is taking shape. One such is Meena Seshu, a young woman of passion, but much more than just a feminist fighting her own corner. It has to be said that she enjoyed telling us how her mother's successful milking herd of water buffaloes had given her an independence which her father had perforce to accept. But her work in investigating the mistreatment of brides and the vexed question of dowry shows clearly her commitment to a balanced family life. Since 1993 she has been at grips with the rise of AIDS and its relationship to prostitution, which is becoming a serious issue in the Sangli district, already resulting in two deaths per week.

Another is Amarsingh Dafle whose pillared family home is the dominant feature of Umrani village. Amarsingh left a possibly more comfortable career in Kirloskar Industries to return to Umrani and farm the family land. He has replanted barren land to forest, which he can remember as a youngster harbouring black buck, not more

163

than thirty or forty years ago. He has built a dam to hold water for irrigation, though the quantity available still remains strictly limited in a dry area. He has, however, been able to launch an area of intensive horticulture which will soon extend to eleven or twelve acres. All this is in fulfilment of a wider vision for the district, which has led him to renew ties with local villagers and seek a way forward for community development.

All in all, Sangli offers solid grounds for hope, and one only has to consider the vast number of NGOs at work in India to realise the impact they are having. Though successive governments have failed to deliver what they might in terms of rural development, these local initiatives have soldiered on. Red tape, setbacks and delays have served only to reinforce a determination to push ahead with even greater vigour. Scientific knowledge and research to fuel the steady acceleration of effort is not lacking. Against this background, the Verala Society stands out both for the quality and durability of its commitment. Perhaps the two go together. Certainly it has shown that it cannot be deflected from its purpose. Nor is there a prospect of riches or influence for those who seek to serve it. Its roots remain with the group of like-minded activists who sought to do something for their locality and for India.

More recently, I have had the chance to see something of another farming development in Bihar, which is part of the outreach from the Tata Industries in Jamshedpur. This is the well-known steel and manufacturing city created by the Tata family in southern Bihar. Right from its founding in the early years of the century, Jamshedpur has been a model city in space and layout, and Tata Industries have been pioneers of worker welfare. Today, with a still-growing emphasis on training, their courses on Human Relations at Work have led to smaller groups being established to continue working out their practical application. A simple example which struck me was a steel worker's conviction to go and look after his brother's farm for a week so that the brother could have a holiday. For holidays have not been part of an Indian farmer's expectation.

Since then, a further step has been taken in recognition of the bridges that need to be built between industry and agriculture. For twelve years now, there has been a company-sponsored initiative for rural development in the villages round the city. Today it covers 400 villages, and is introducing water conservation, irrigation and multiple cropping on land which had been stagnating with a single rain-fed rice crop.

Dorkasai village, and my friend Shailendra Mahato, are symbolic of this change. In the first wave of advance, the village was passed over, because help was offered only to those who sought it with a united aim in mind. Shailendra was at daggers drawn with Thakurdas Mahato, a political rival for village leadership. Shailendra is an Adivasi (aboriginal) and was a member of the militant Jharkhand Party, which campaigns for a separate state for the Adivasis. His bitterness against the Biharis began when he went to study in Jamshedpur, and was so much bullied that he ended by packing in his studies. His hatred was further fuelled when he was promised a job in Tata's Telco factory, but had it withdrawn by the department head because of the violence with which he had led mobs against encroachment on Adivasi land. In 1982, he went to a seminar in Jamshedpur in the place of a cousin who had refused the invitation. Although satisfied he was already providing leadership to the exploited class, and had not much to learn, he did not dismiss out of hand the idea of listening to the inner voice for direction.

It was in such a time of listening that his own need to change became clear to him. His first conviction was to give more time to his wife and apologise for his neglect of her. She was having difficulty in her relationship with his mother, a common situation where the extended family is living together under one roof. Despite her sceptical reception to begin with, they became able to share what they felt without rancour, and so to begin to find answers. Next Shailendra apologised to his political rival for his bitterness towards him. They found that, even with different political opinions, they could unite in seeking what was right for village development.

At this point, Shailendra was under financial pressure and thinking of looking for a job. But his new friends were urging him to consider irrigating his land and developing his seven acres. It was then, in 1987, that I first came to his village, having been invited to see his farm. He showed me the lie of the land, and where he hoped to make a pond for irrigation water and to raise fish. In 1993, I was back again, and able to see what had been accomplished. A pond, first dug by hand, had been enlarged with the help of a mechanical digger from Telco (a Tata company). It now measured 370 feet by 275 feet and 15 feet deep. It contained several species of fish, which were netted and restocked annually. Potatoes and mustard followed the rice crop, plus an assortment of vegetables, while 10 or 11 more ponds had been dug, and cropping was being extended on other farms. It was an enormous encouragement to see how the vision had been realised, and further plans were already in mind to set up a cooperative, both for buying inputs and marketing produce. There is also the further possibility of a cooperative dairy herd of 25 water buffalos to produce milk for sale in the city.

On this same occasion, I was present for a village meeting organised to welcome P N Pandey, the head of Tata's rural development work. It was addressed by Shailendra, Thakurdas, his former political opponent, and another friend, and it was impressive to hear how a new spirit could bear so much fruit for the community. There were two new schools to be seen, one a repaired and rebuilt primary school, and the other a brand new secondary school almost ready for occupation.

I reflected on a statement at this time by Indian Secretary of Agriculture, M S Gill, that 'There's no way you can reach the Eighth Plan target unless you step up production in areas like Eastern Uttar Pradesh and Bihar.' This referred to the aim of raising total production of food grains to 210 million tons by 1996/7 from the then current level close to 180 million tons. It was also necessary to raise Government procurement from 6.5 million tons to a possible 9-10 million tons to meet the needs of those who buy food from the

Government's Fair Price shops (an important scheme for those too poor to buy at market prices, because it avoids depressing the prices to the farmer). In commenting on these needs, Gill remarked that much more could not be expected of the Punjab, where the greatest contribution had already been made and yields were high. For, whatever the criticisms of the Green Revolution, the standard of living in the Punjab is 50% higher than the average for all India.

In the same drive for modernisation, the National Dairy Development Board, responsible for what is sometimes dubbed the White Revolution, has been criticised for being too high tech and for selling expensive milk to the well-heeled customers in the big cities. This is to misunderstand its purpose, which was to develop a commercial market for small milk producers in the many areas a long way from the centres of population. 'It had its origins in a strike of milk producers against a private firm given monopoly rights by the Bombay Provincial Government in 1946. Under enlightened political tutelage, the striking milk producers formed a co-operative and eventually won for it the right also to collect milk in the district and sell it to the Government. They started with an initial collection of just 250 litres' (official brochure).

Operation Flood itself dated from 1970 and was aimed at replicating the Anand Cooperative pattern. 'Since its inception in 1970, Operation Flood has extended to 173 milk-sheds around the country. Some 6.5 million farm households are members of 60,000 village dairy cooperatives. Of the farm families covered, 21% have no land, another 66% are small and marginal farmers owning less than four hectares of land. Only 10% of the families own more than four milk animals so Operation Flood in practice has been a development programme aimed at improving the lot of the less privileged rural peasant' (*From a Drip to a Flood*, 1990).

It is important to understand this, because Operation Flood is an example of the successful and creative application of food aid. Butter oil and milk powder from the European Community, fed into the system through recombining plants, have helped to even out supplies around the year, and to stabilise prices to the producer, while the money generated from the commercial sale of this aid has financed the steady expansion of the co-operative enterprise. In that sense, the aid has been truly used by the recipient country to generate further development and increase its self-reliance. So it is a very good example of the realisation of all the hopes which had been placed upon it.

At every stage, the farmers have employed professionals to do the management, and they have been extraordinarily well served. Criticisms of stainless steel and modern dairy technology seem irrelevant when you consider how else fresh milk could be delivered and successfully distributed in cities like Bombay, Delhi and Calcutta; farmers will be impressed that the producer has consistently received at least 70% of the price paid by the consumer. It is a record of which anyone could be proud.

The outline of this story has been given because it has been the subject of much needless controversy. But it may also be that it mirrors a wider division in the world of development, where principles are often laid down and defended, when what matters is the actual outcome in the field. There can be no question that grass-roots development at village level, demonstrated by the work of numerous NGOs and private initiatives, is the type of indigenous growth that is needed. It keeps the growth and the action firmly in the farmers' own hands. Yet it should be equally clear that the Anand Cooperative started from similar beginnings but has grown into a national initiative perhaps without precedent. Certainly it has attracted the interest of other Asian countries which would be only too glad to emulate it.

That the control remains constitutionally in the hands of the farmers concerned is undoubtedly due to Dr Kurien (first Director of Operation Flood and later of the National Dairy Development Board) and his staff. They may be criticised for their mistakes, but they cannot be faulted for the quality of their commitment. For this reason alone, they represent a balance between the farmer on the ground and the consumer in the city, which must still have plenty of mileage in it. This is not to regard it as some sort of potential monopoly, because there are and will be many other approaches in a country with India's diversity. But as well as a multitude of small operations, there also need to be some operations of real magnitude in a country of India's scale. That they should keep the farmer in the forefront of the picture is, of course, every farmer's prayer.

Tata Industries have lessons to offer here as well. The smaller groups already mentioned pursue the application of the ideas given in the main seminars. They are at grips with the question of how to create something new in society which puts industry in its true perspective. I was interested to hear a story about J R D Tata – the late patriarch of the company – which brought this home to me. Someone had been expatiating to him on their forward vision, and how India could easily become a future 'economic superpower'. Tata is said to have commented later, 'I don't want India to become an "economic superpower", I just want India to be a happy country.'

Such a basic conviction must have lain behind the story of Santal Mahato in a village out in the wild from Jamshedpur, which I had the good fortune to visit. He was the first student from his village to graduate in higher education, and he went to the city in search of a job. Some of those he met at Tata suggested to him that if he came to the city he would be one among a multitude, but in his own village he could be a pioneer, and organise his own school. He went away, pondered on this suggestion and decided to pursue it.

When I visited his village in February 1993, only seven years later, there was a flourishing school of 135 pupils with three teachers. But even more remarkable was the spirit in which it had grown. It was a Sunday, and although the children were not at school, a selection of villagers and staff had gathered to welcome us, and also, as they evidently did quite often, to assess progress. Since we were late arriving, they employed their time in writing a traditional ballad about a young man and his mother-in-law, which they proceeded to sing to us on our arrival!

Santal himself is a young man of quiet and gentle character, who might seem, at first sight, an unlikely leader for such an enterprise. But in its tranquillity and isolation, the village has a special atmosphere in which the development could take place with a certain uninterrupted innocence.

As we talked, one former student related his experience in stealing stones from the forest, which is all around. To us, it seemed a comparatively harmless activity on the side, and one was inclined to marvel that such stone could find a ready market. But it transpired that contracts for stone were a major source of income to the Government Forestry Service. Since it was determined to crack down on a widespread activity, our friend found himself billed for 30,000 Rupees. He gave a graphic account of the emotions this aroused in him, including the fear of imminent imprisonment, while his comrades frequently rocked with laughter. Finally he had found the courage to go to the forester, admit what he had done and apologise. Needless to say the value of what he had taken was probably only a fraction of the 30,000 rupees, and the forest officer readily forgave him. In fact, he commented how rare it was to find anyone honestly admitting to any wrong-doing, and became a firm friend of the school from then on.

Another former pupil recounted with equal verve how frequently and successfully he and his brother had played truant from the school. Keeping within sound of the school bell, they knew when lessons were over, and made their way self-righteously home for the meal. As hard-working students, they expected to get the biggest helping of whatever was on the menu. Their long and successful run only came to an end when a neighbour spotted them one day and told their parents. But the point he wanted to make was how much he regretted the wasted opportunity, and to urge the present generation not to fritter it away.

Again the story was punctuated with much laughter, and it struck me how intensely people lived into the everyday life of the village. They followed these blow-by-blow stories so closely because they were the reality of village life. There was a simplicity and sometimes a certain ingenuousness, but also a clarity that was leading them to a creative power which was evident in their understanding together.

Another man to speak was one of the teachers, who hoped shortly to see his exploits in the *Guinness Book of Records*. He had been involved with three others in a non-stop rafting record along 2400kms of river. But besides recounting some of his adventures, he spoke of how he took his class into the forest to be quiet with nature and to listen to the inner voice. He observed how much better they concentrated in class as a result.

All this might seem a far cry from more sophisticated societies with their plethora of problems, but to me it is a parable of the true India. It is a source of wonder that, wherever you go, the authority of the inner voice seems to be recognised by all classes and by all creeds or no creed. It is part of the truth that keeps India one nation through all its diversities and divisions. What is more, for the majority, it appears to be seen as the voice of God rather than merely the voice of conscience.

Faced with the need for moral and spiritual rearmament in a divided and sometimes violent society, this is an enormous strength. Indians combine with it a sense of their birthright of freedom, which is firmly based on individual responsibility. That is a foundation for brotherhood and integration which may yet belie the communal riots, and put compassion into the campaign against poverty.

Farmers internationally would rejoice to see the hundreds of millions of peasant farmers in Asia enter a new era and find a voice through organisation. For although many political leaders have sprung from the heart of village life, there is not yet a generally accepted and recognised body of professional farmers.

Some of the misgivings aroused by the GATT negotiations were expressed by Dr G C Mahanta, Agricultural Director of Tata's Rural Development round Jamshedpur (letter, November 1993). 'Agriculture being the mainstay and providing stability for our country, should mean that commensurate status is given to the farmers by a concerned Government. Modern critical inputs should be made available in suitable locations for the poor farmers of India. The agricultural prices should be protected by the Government at all cost.' This underlines the point that agriculture must first grow strong, before farmers are not only able to compete but also to fight their own corner in the international arena. Both India and China have vast resources of manpower which can bring muscle to their industrial development, but full employment may depend on the prosperity of a labour-intensive farming which has yet to find its true pattern.

If anything, China presents the bigger question-mark. For the Peoples' Republic of China is the other vast Asian country where farmers are to be numbered in the hundreds of millions. Their record in feeding the country is also a proud one, and since the end of the Cultural Revolution they have played a vital role in the proliferation of new initiatives which have resulted in spectacular economic expansion. Since I haven't myself had the opportunity of a visit there, I draw my information from a paper entitled 'Rural China and Chinese farmers on their way to a market economy.' This was prepared for the international Farmers' Dialogue at Caux in Switzerland in January 1994 by Professor Gao Lu, editor of *The Economic Daily* in Beijing and his wife Professor Zhang Guilin of the University of Politics and Law in Beijing.

It makes the point that the farmers themselves were responsible for the present Household Contracted Responsibility System, which for the first time linked remuneration with output on the basis of an individual household responsibility. The Party's Central Committee had approved a responsibility system that included the fixing of output quotas on the basis of production groups, and remuneration linked to output, but had forbidden the fixing of such quotas on the basis of individual households and individual farming.

The enthusiasm of a group of farmers in Anhui province led them to break this injunction. A dozen households in Xiaogang village shared out the land to individual households on their own initiative, and signed or fingerprinted a responsibility contract among themselves. When this action came to the attention of the local authorities, Wan Li, the Party Secretary for Anhui Province, tacitly approved their action. The result is that today this contract is preserved as an historic document, so great were the changes for which it paved the way.

Almost unwittingly, the farmers had opened a new road for development. Their spirit, in operating on the basis of individual households at the risk of being put in prison, attracted the attention of China's top leaders. It wasn't long before they saw the virtues of making the system the basis of a nationwide pattern. In the space of the next five years, over 90% of all production teams had implemented the policy. It heralded a fundamental reform in the economic structure of agricultural management in rural China. It was accompanied by a rapid growth in agricultural production which fully proved its worth. Indeed, to underline it, some farmers in 1984 even had problems in marketing their produce amid the ample supplies from a good harvest.

Since 80% of China's population live in rural areas, a surplus rural labour force has posed a serious problem. The answer has been to encourage the surplus labourers to plant more non-food crops, to increase forestry, animal breeding, fisheries and other sideline occupations that make up a diversified economy.

Various forms of 'specialised households' and households engaging in industrial or commercial businesses have come to the fore, heralding a readjustment of agricultural structure in rural China. Small workshops of different trades sprang up first, and grew into small factories or co-operative associations on the basis of individual households or the extended family clan. Based on the commune-run or brigade-owned enterprises, townships and villages began to establish a large number of industrial ventures. By 1988, the gross value of the output of the non-agricultural sectors was 53% against 47% for agriculture. This was the first time in Chinese history that such a balance had been struck.

By the end of 1993 value of the output of industry in rural areas was 50% of China's total industrial output. This expansion of industrial activity is a phenomenon created by the Chinese farmers, and even Deng Xiaoping admitted that he had 'never expected that'. Raw materials and finished products are all traded on the free market, so have to be competitive to survive. But such a rapid transformation has called for considerable mental readjustment and the need to develop a fresh philosophy about the rural way of life.

In parenthesis to the paper of Professors Gao and Zhang, it is reported that China is losing nearly one million hectares, or 1% of its cropping area per year to industrialisation, and looks like following a similar path to Japan, South Korea and Taiwan, where grain areas have reduced from 8 million hectares to 4 million hectares in the last 30 years. Professor Zhou Guangzhao, head of the Chinese Academy of Sciences, observed early in 1994 that if the nation continues to squander its farmland and water resources in a breakneck effort to industrialise, 'then China will have to import 400 million tons of grain by 2030. And I am afraid, in that case, that all the grain output of the USA could not meet China's needs.' Such a conflict of interest is bound to create tensions. Competitive enterprises seek greater efficiency, and the main goal of business is to gain the largest profits. In a sense, this view of life is quite alien to traditional ideas derived from Confucian philosophy, and is not easily assimilated.

This is a theme developed by Professors Gao and Zhang in their paper. They note that a new view of things, still based on traditional ethics, is now beginning to take shape among the Chinese farmers. Confucius once said, 'It is man's desire to make profits and become rich, but you must not make money in an unjust way'. Today, the idea is taking root of 'becoming rich through honest labour,' and 'thinking of generosity in attitudes when making profits'. To build up the family fortunes in a civilised way is seen as perfectly consistent with spiritual values and even socialist ideals.

A great deal remains to be tackled. There is a widening gap between incomes in industry and agriculture, and a similar gap between rural areas in different parts of the country. In broad terms, the per-capita income in East China's rural areas is more than twice that of those in the West. And the slow pace of urbanisation has delayed the transfer of surplus labour from rural areas to the cities, though there is strong pressure to jump the gun.

Progress can be measured by the fact that until 1978 there were still some 100 million people in rural China who were short of both food and clothing. By the end of 1993 that figure was down to 26 million, though of course there are vastly more whose income is still well below FAO's official definition of poverty. The encouraging point is that the Chinese Government continues to pay close attention to the development of rural society and the rural economy.

The paper ends with a declaration of the farmers' confidence that they will conquer new heights. But while no-one would question that confidence, one wonders where it may lead in terms of farmers' international solidarity, and the way we must work together. The GATT agreement, so painfully concluded with a first-time incorporation of agriculture needs, should soon have Chinese participation. The World Trade Organisation might even become a genuine multilateral forum for fair trade practice. That would at least be in line with Confucius. But there are some things in human society that lie beyond the reach of the political process, and are not cured by prosperity.

Among them are the wounds of body and spirit inflicted by civil war or by the injustices of an unfeeling authority intent on maintaining law and order. To heal and to forgive is not an easy path to follow. Britain is learning that, in the quest for peace in Ireland, it is necessary to face both the wrongs of the past and the desire for control in the present. She does not yet have the answer, any more than India does in Kashmir or China in Tibet. These are human tragedies which can only be healed in the spirit. An Irish Catholic farmer said not long ago 'We have every right to take up arms against a foreign power to attain a united Ireland'. The pity is that many Protestant farmers in Ulster scarcely seemed to recognise 25 years ago that such opinions were firmly and passionately held. As has sometimes been remarked before, in Ireland the feelings are the facts. But Ireland is not alone in that.

Here again, Confucius may have something to contribute, as I am learning from studying a translation of the Analects. Confucius believed that, in order to meet his moral responsibility, a man must think for himself. This led him to place as much emphasis on thinking as on learning, and his philosophy is embodied in an ideal man whose virtues are reflected in his actions. For Confucius, as apparently for the whole of the Chinese tradition, politics is only an extension of morals: provided that the ruler is benevolent, the government will naturally work towards the good of the people. He comments that even with a true king, it is bound to take a generation for benevolence to become a reality. 'If a man cannot make himself correct, what business has he with making others correct? ' In those days, so much depended on the character of the ruler that the common man was only expected to be a follower, whether for lack of opportunity or lack of capacity to shoulder responsibility. However, Confucius shrewdly declares, 'The three armies can be deprived of their commanding officer, but even a common man cannot be deprived of his purpose'.

He also underlines the importance of commitment in helping others. 'A benevolent man helps others to take their stand in so far as he himself wishes to take his stand, and gets others there in so far as he himself wishes to go there. The ability to take an analogy which is near at hand (viz oneself) can be called the method of benevolence.'

India and China are the two massive centres of population in Asia, and their peoples are also to be found playing a prominent part in other countries. Would they together provide an unassailable bulwark for progress, if a real trust between them could be built? There is much talk about the established and emerging economies of the Pacific Rim but, in the longer term, the region's stability will rest on the mutual understanding of her peoples. Since agriculture will remain a dominant activity, and adequate food supplies cannot be taken for granted, it would seem that the farmers have a growing part to play. They may have yet to find their voice, but when they do, it will surely be heard. Those who hope for the great truths of Asian culture to be a power in the next century are looking a long way beyond the Pacific Rim. It could be a good moment to consider seriously the potential of a farmers' world network.

Chapter 16
A Farmers' World Network

The starting point in this chapter is an organisation which has actually become known as the Farmer's World Network, based in the National Agricultural Centre at Stoneleigh. Of recent origin (1985) it is, hopefully, still young enough not to have become set in its ways. For that is essential if it is to fulfil the vision of its founders and become a body which flowers in the 21st century. For the moment it is in its formative and pioneering phase.

Some things develop through careful planning and others, like Topsy, are said to have 'just growed'. Perhaps it doesn't matter too much how things start to shape up, and whether people get it right first time. That tends to be the judgement of the age we live in, and certainly the important thing is the impulse which gets things moving. There is ample time to shape up along the road, providing there is a minimum of prejudice and preconception concealed in the baggage. So when the question of a coordinating network was raised, there were already a variety of initiatives in the field. Some of them found their way into the Network and some didn't, or haven't done so far. This means there is a wide range of approaches to consider, and still some way to go in catching the farmers' interest and focusing on what farmers would like to achieve.

The Farmers' Third World Network, as it was originally called, arose in response to the publicity given to the famine in Ethiopia in 1984. Aidan Harrison, a Northumberland sheep and cattle farmer, wrote an article (*Farmers Weekly*, November 1984) commenting on the irrational nature of agricultural policies world-wide. This stimulated a small group of farmers to meet in January 1985 to discuss how they might respond in coordination with NGOs already in the field.

Joseph Rocher of RONGEAD (A European network started in 1983) in giving the parallel French experience, emphasised the importance of direct farmer-to-farmer links. He pointed out that personal contact is a very important motor for increasing understanding and changing ideas. Tony Hill of the Catholic Institute for International Relations mentioned some of the differences between France and the UK, explaining that the NGOs had yet to make a relationship with the farmers in Britain. He suggested that the farmers might have three possible relations with the NGOs.

1 They might join the NGOs as individuals.
2 The NGOs might take the initiative and produce material for them as a constituency.
3 The NGOs might try to take the role of supporting the farmers – on the farmers' initiative.

With hindsight, it is perhaps the third of these possibilities which has failed to materialise as it might have done. Farmer-to-farmer initiatives had already been the subject of an investigation by the Centre for Agricultural Strategy, then headed by Professor Sir Colin Spedding, who enlisted the help of Andrew Korbey, formerly of Unilever. Their subject was the Brandt Report and UK agriculture, which also raised the question of coordinated action. They urged that the various aid groups should come together, not for fund-raising or operation, but to address the public with one voice. Professor Spedding argued that the public needed a clear and combined voice on the overall needs, so that agencies were seen to be 'getting their act together' and relating what each did to the work of others.

In the course of this investigation, Andrew Korbey was able to identify some twenty groups engaged in farmer-to-farmer links overseas. He encouraged them to think of meeting together, and also arranged some publicity in the *Farmers' Weekly* (January 1984). So it was from this initiative that our Herefordshire group was invited to participate in a formative meeting in Birmingham (November 1985), which followed the first national meeting of the Network group in London (May 1985).

At the outset, the main thrust of the initiative to build a co-ordinating body came from people working in the development field, particularly those returning from Voluntary Service Overseas. This was reflected in the fact that the most useful work done at the beginning was in awakening an interest in such studies at agricultural colleges. These studies are now established, and have been reinforced by a growing number of international contacts. It has led to a successful application for funding from the European Union, and the subsequent appointment of a full-time Coordinator. But the progress made in development education and environmental issues has not so far been matched by farmer involvement.

Here it is perhaps worth considering individual cases. I have referred to our Farmers' Group in Herefordshire at some length in the chapter on India. This consists of about a dozen families, and sees itself as essentially a house group including wives as fully as husbands, and able to meet in a farmhouse sitting room. So far, we have sailed under the flag of British Farmers for International Development, in the hope that such moves in Britain could parallel the initiatives that created AFDI in France (Agriculteurs Français et Developpement International). This hope has not been fulfilled, but it has not prevented our Herefordshire group from advancing a long way down the road towards the goals it set itself. On the way, it has created farmer-to-farmer links not only in India but also in Thailand and Poland.

The first thing British farmers have to learn, as mentioned earlier, is to master some of the basics of farming in a tropical or semi-tropical climate. Once these differences are taken on board, it is possible to enter into the local situation, and seek to understand the hopes and aspirations of the farmers. They may already have projects under consideration, but often it is helpful to absorb the climate of local opinion without any preconceptions or plans. Then one can truly share in development as it grows, rather than as it is fostered by grants or other aids that seek to steer in a particular direction. Such a process can be more important than the time it takes, which to Westerners is so often seen as a vital measure of progress.

From our group's standpoint, there is clearly sometimes a tension between fund-raising and exploring common professional interests in technology, farming practice or marketing. We are a small-budget operation, partly reflecting our own financial circumstances, but also because we have not wanted money-raising to dominate our programme. This is not to say that we wouldn't welcome more substantial gifts, or that we cannot see useful ways of spending a great deal more! Rather it is because we are conscious that the value of development cannot be measured in financial terms, and many extremely valuable local advances cost very little. Furthermore, our basic search is for new leadership and new patterns, in what is destined to be a very comprehensive commitment extending to all aspects of a farmer's way of life. Men and women of integrity and vision are not so easily come by and, when discovered, the greatest help may be found in a comradeship of purpose, which surprisingly enough can unite the comparatively affluent western farmers with the peasant farmers of Asia and Africa.

This quest has also been pursued by our neighbours in Worcestershire, who operate as the Farmers Overseas Action Group (FOAG) in Uganda. From time to time we have compared notes, and our shared experience has been that the personal approach and the friendships made have been both the real satisfaction and the practical guarantee of future developments. FOAG, with a budget which now tops £25,000 per annum, has felt the need to put the brakes on financial expansion so that the tail does not begin to wag the dog and faithful activists get taken over by an initiative that was never intended to become a major business.

FOAG has worked a good deal with Voluntary Service Overseas, backing volunteers in situations which they have discovered to be in need of help. This has worked well, and enabled continuity to be maintained in a way that is difficult from outside. It has to be emphasised, however, that members of the group have been very faithful in managing visits every year. Hopefully, it will become easier to get to know Ugandans who can take over the work of the volunteers, and establish a true partnership. It has already become clear that education must be at the forefront of all development, and one of the Worcester group's most rewarding initiatives has been with an orphanage at Masindi. The orphanage has a substantial farm attached, and is run by Livingstone Barongo, who has poured himself out for the children in his care. The years of civil war in Uganda have resulted in a cruelly large number of orphans in the country and, from the President downwards, serious and sustained efforts have been made to give them the opportunities and training of which they have been deprived. Many respond with a dedication that may well lead them to make contributions to their country far beyond the call of duty. In this respect, it is disappointing that people still so often see development in terms of projects rather than of people. Both Hereford and Worcester groups have experienced how much easier it is to raise money for a concrete project than to gain backing for a group of people committed to a local programme that may be worthy in the long term but unspectacular in its gestation. This may be connected to the old saying that some people would rather pay than pray. But it is certainly true that those who become personally involved and give of themselves and their own time and experience are meeting a real human need.

That is really what 'networking' should be about. Even in our jargonised world, I was a little surprised to find the word has become so quickly incorporated into the language, though it does suggest a certain way of approaching things. There again, some may see it in terms of people and others in terms of organisation, to promote co-operation and eliminate overlapping. Suffice it to say that, in a non-commercial relationship, unselfishness can have full play and that, once there is trust, mutual understanding can grow by leaps and bounds.

The Ministry of Agriculture in Uganda runs a scheme for regional farm competitions throughout the country. Intended to identify the most capable and go-ahead farmers, their prize is a fortnight's trip to the UK. It is a chance to see farms and visit the Royal Show. So it is interesting that the minister has chosen FOAG to host these occasions, because she had the opportunity to know them and their work before joining the Government.

This illustrates the way things can begin to knit together, because it is not enough simply to foster an alternative agenda to the way things are being done at present. In so far as such a concept has taken root among some NGOs, it must surely be mistaken. For if development means anything, it must mean a convergence on a world goal. That means change for the whole of society: rich and poor, powerful and powerless. Anything less will only compound the problems to be overcome.

A certain consensus has emerged in the last 10-20 years on lessons which have been learned by hard experience. Such basic truths cover points like the relative importance of agriculture in a nation's economy, the scope for farmers to control their own destiny, their role in scientific trials and research, and the extent to which farming and conservation should march hand in hand. All these are farmers' issues, and peasant farmers frequently express opinions on them which never reach any public forum. That is perhaps where a change of attitude most needs to be fostered, and where farmer-to-farmer links often bring their influence to bear. Personal friendships which are intended to be for life can have the staying power which is needed. They foster a depth of understanding which covers not only the logistics of the situation but the outlook of the local farmers and their sense of the role they can play in the economic and political life of their country. It is common for farmers organisations like IFAP (International Federation of Agricultural Producers) to bemoan the fact that farmers have been consulted so little by governments in deliberations about agricultural issues; and they complain not without reason. Yet it is only comparatively recently that farmers have got fully involved in such matters themselves, and that IFAP has launched its programme of helping the development of farmers' organisations in member countries. All the same, it is surprising that, a year before the UN conference on Environment and Development at Rio in 1992, agriculture was not even on the agenda. It quickly became the largest chapter in the so-called Agenda 21, which focuses on the next century.

In this connection, it is interesting to note the activities of the NFU, which took over the 'send a tonne to Africa' grain programme initiated by Oliver Walston after the Ethiopian famine of 1984. I had imagined that this was conceived as a one-off response to crisis, and that it was not intended to get involved in long term development. But it struck a real chord and, perhaps inevitably, developed its own momentum. The NFU reacted by deciding to back two projects in Ethiopia already launched by different NGOs. But not surprisingly, the first impulse to give generously could not be sustained. This led to a reappraisal and a switch to backing 'Farm Africa' which offered a more personal approach, focusing at the outset on a very grass-roots programme with camels and goats. It also aimed exclusively at empowering those on the ground to undertake their own improvements.

Even so, the first approach to chairmen of County Milk Committees drew a number of negative reactions, based on the rather short-sighted view that this sort of thing was not within the field of NFU business. Perhaps again this was due to the fact that the emphasis was more on raising money than personal involvement, though Lord Plumb weighed in with the thought that 'send a son' might be more relevant than 'send a tonne'.

'Farm Africa' is now establishing itself as the industry's particular charitable enterprise and pursuing a pattern of farmer-directed thinking which puts a high value on indigenous leadership. Many World Network members are active in its support. But while the need for fund-raising inevitably looms large in the activities it undertakes in the UK, its underlying thought about Africa may yet prove more significant in the long run. It aims to build up committed professional support through an understanding of what is happening on the ground. It is all part of an approach which will sooner or later bring a world network into the realm of practical politics. With the speeding up of democratic processes everywhere, it is an interesting question at what point government and grass-roots moves will meet and integrate.

That is not to say that they do not meet already, but there are great gaps both in mutual understanding and relative strengths in different parts of the world. Farmers overall, though making great strides in a wide range of local situations, are still more planned-for than planning for themselves. So it is interesting to hear the new leaders of Eritrea declare, 'Although poor, we wish to be self-reliant and not to go down the usual road of debt and dependency to the donors of the West'. Their conviction is echoed by the BBC's 'Own Correspondent' who reported: 'I have never seen such a highly-motivated population… The long years of sacrifice and civil war have produced a determination to create a country that is worth living in' (March 1996).

To match the challenge of such a commitment in the international field, a common purpose needs to be identified. Even the NFU is sometimes criticised by its rank-and-file for its expenditure on the IFAP and, as late as the summer of 1994, there were murmurs of dismay that three delegates should have been sent to the conference in Turkey. It was seen by the critics simply as a junket at the expense of members, rather than a chance to further the cause of farming solidarity. So clearly the network's motivation cannot be taken for granted either.

The difficulty here is that the spiritual values, which sustain so many in face of the materialism of the age we live in, can be mistrusted if they are thought to include some of the wilder flights of idealism or even too much dogma. The more so if such tendencies diverge from the core business of earning a living and raising a family to participate in society, and seem to divert into some semi-heroic alternative. But this is a point at which wider historical forces will also have to be weighed in the balance, as we consider farming's contribution to the great issues of the next century, the closing of the rich-poor gap and the establishment of democratic values worldwide.

Back in April 1994, two items of news appeared simultaneously in the press. One recorded the ANC's commitment after the South African elections to see that 30% of the agricultural land was occupied by black farmers by the end of the century. The other recorded the Russian Government's decision that the land of 27,000 collective farms was now legally available for purchase and private farming. Both present a supreme challenge to the climate of opinion in the countries involved. Both represent a fundamental change of direction. But it could be a mistake to imagine that we as outside observers already know the kind of development which is needed.

In 1992, Ben Boughton, formerly a well-known farmer in the pig world, was one of those who went on a feasibility study in South Africa on behalf of Farm Africa. He wrote this in *Landmark* (July/August 1995).

Wherever we travelled we stressed to our hosts – whites, blacks and coloureds alike – that Farm Africa has no agricultural expertise which is not already available in South Africa. They all replied, 'You are needed because here the races are unable to talk to each other, and this will endure for a generation. Because of your record in East Africa, all will be willing to work with you.' We spent three days in the coloured homelands in the far north of Cape Province. Our host there was Noel Williams of the Kasigo Trust. As an active opponent of apartheid, Noel had spent most of the 1980s in prison, and the account which he gave me of the degrading treatment to which he had been subjected was harrowing. At length I said to him, 'Noel, if I had been asked to show a white man around for three days, I should have told my boss where he could stuff the white man'. His reply will remain with me for ever. 'Ben, if we bear rancour, there will never be a new South Africa; if we can forgive and forget, there is just a chance that there will be a new South Africa.' This was the first time I had come across that tremendous spirit of reconciliation which nowadays, nearly three years later, seems to be the norm.

Revisiting South Africa in 1995 the changes which have occurred are quite remarkable, and although massive problems remain, the replacement of foreboding by optimism is truly amazing. Not least remarkable among the changes is that some of the formerly most intransigent Afrikaaners now seem to be enthusiastic converts to this new system... If any overseas development agency is to do its job properly, its eventual objective must be to make itself redundant. Our principal reason for going to South Africa was in response to the widely-held view that the different races would be unable to work with each other for a generation. But the pace of change and reconciliation has been such that it may not be too much to hope that in five years Farm Africa's presence may no longer be necessary.

It is a sobering thought that changes can take place in men's hearts so speedily, even if much more is still needed. Can we become so deeply involved with the problems of others as to share their search for a satisfying way of life? It is perhaps only the logic of declaring, as we frequently do, that we live in an interdependent world. A world view is not only possible, but has got to become practical. It will not be practised through the elaboration of some gigantic blueprint but through individual decisions.

Farmer-to-farmer links, at their most basic, are the network of friendships which arise between neighbours and colleagues with shared interests. Many who, during their working lives, are precluded from much travel hesitate to get involved further afield. But in recent years, holidays have become more frequent, and more exotic destinations have been entertained, even if sometimes regarded as once-in-a-lifetime occasions. Pushed beyond the Channel into Europe, or across the world, such links open new dimensions of policy, and could play a decisive part in the next century.

They could be part of the drive for a new definition of farming's professional status, and a road to fulfilment for those coming out of agricultural colleges intending to devote themselves to becoming farmers. One such, who is highly successful in the horticultural field, wrote to me recently, 'I think the challenge for my generation is to remove economics from being leader', ie from its domination in the business of living. That is in essence a call to roll back materialism, and establish an economy which meets human need, ending the North/South divergence. It is not too much to hope that it can be done through networks of people who commit themselves to such a purpose, but it will require a transformation in attitudes that is lifelong and far-reaching. It is unlikely to be accomplished in a single generation, but its realisation could be rapid once there is an inner acceptance of the need.

Whether the Farmers' World Network conceives itself in such a role remains to be seen. Certainly it does not accept that the so-called 'developed' countries are in less need of change than the 'developing' countries. For the present, it awaits a consultant's report on the best way to adjust its strategy and focus its goals. But however clear the analysis of the present, a lot of uncharted water lies ahead. Progress will depend on the degree of unity which can be brought to the task of navigation.

Chapter 17
What Now?

So far as our present efforts are concerned, it would seem that the WTO is destined to remain one of the pillars around which policy revolves. At the same time, we must remember that on a world basis the vast bulk of food is consumed in the country which produced it, and the major need of the moment is to establish and strengthen domestic agriculture throughout the poorer countries. This is necessary not just to ward off famine and food shortage, but to nourish the health and strength of peoples who seek a new life and a full destiny.

A discussion document from the NFU (England and Wales) entitled 'Real Choices' set out very well the options on offer for the next stage in the reform of the CAP. Some would say it needs to be a total resurrection to a new life but there is also a surprising amount of basic agreement on broad aims. First, export subsidies need to be not only reduced but abolished, and this means the end of price support through intervention buying, though there is a strong case for organised reserve stocks. Then a more sober judgement can be made on marrying up environmental needs with the patterns of domestic production. To do this, the most attractive option would seem to be 'decoupling', which, although it remains to be costed, gives maximum flexibility by separating subsidy payments from the support of price levels. The basic argument for this is that it clears the way for the emergence of world price levels which have a true relationship with costs of production.

Whether world price levels would rise for cereals remains to be seen, but margins have been tight even for the lowest-cost producers. In Australia, for example, there is a rising interest in conservation, which suggests a pressure and a desire to face up to environmental questions where climate cannot easily be taken for granted. This, of course, is now to be an integral part of the considerations to be covered by the WTO, though no-one knows yet exactly how it will work out. Since the small staff employed on the agricultural side of the WTO can scarcely be expected to make a judgement on these matters, it will probably be left in most cases for the consumer to decide. This would apply both to scientific judgements, such as the use of hormones in beef production, and to more contentious judgements on the sustainability of production systems in the country of origin. Clearly, in these campaigning days, truth will sometimes be a casualty. But at least the process will be conducted in public, and will provide another area in which farmers must establish a closer and stronger relationship with their customers.

It could also be said that, while enlargement of the European Union has been dictated by political rather than economic considerations, it may prove a timely help in considering what is the best way to achieve a more open agricultural policy. Everyone is looking for outlets for their production and, if you ask Polish farmers how the West can help, it will not be long before someone suggests that the best help would be to open our markets to their produce. There may be a breathing space before this becomes acute, but it will be the inevitable end of the reform processes which are now in evolution throughout Central and Eastern Europe. At the same time, with world grain stocks at their lowest for over twenty years, the scenario has shifted from surplus to scarcity. Rising world populations need to be fed, and we cannot afford to look to the future in terms of past experience.

We do, in fact, stand at the parting of the ways, not just for farmers but for the whole range of human society. Farmers who feel themselves to be battling for survival may find it hard to believe that they could lead the way. We have got used to the idea that power has shifted to industrial development, and that our main job is to see that we are not entirely swamped. But when it appears that even the largest companies have feet of clay, individuals must again take heart. It may not be vanity to suppose that farming can produce leadership of real calibre, even if today many of its most successful practitioners avoid the public stage.

Happily, there are very few precedents to guide us, which may make it easier to strike out in a new direction. Above all else must be the conviction that farming has a great deal to offer, and is more about making a good living and a good life than creating millionaires. Bound up with this is the aim of full employment. No one supposes that we can live indefinitely with the current levels of unemployment, but the goal of full employment has receded in people's minds as an attainable objective. Quite a lot has been done to foster alternative employment in rural areas, but it still remains an assumption that agriculture itself is destined to go on losing manpower into the far future. What a blessing if such assumptions could prove unfounded! Yet such changes do not come by chance, but only from conviction and as the fruit of a committed purpose.

Now may well be the moment to try to forge such a purpose, when the WTO has entered the agricultural scene and the challenge of a wider Europe has been thrust to the fore. Pedro Camargo Neto, the Brazilian farmers' President, put a common complaint into words when he said, 'We cannot turn a blind eye to the way the agreement (GATT) was negotiated. The negotiating posture went against a fundamental principle - multilateralism. The weak nations' positions were practically ignored. The strong ones made it clear that they were the nations in control, and that those with any common sense should follow their lead. The power demonstrated by both the United States and the European Union, in our view, endangers the principle of consensus and proper negotiation, which should guide all business standards.'

Great changes might result from such a fresh approach. In April 1994, the popular Brazilian Presidential candidate Luiz 'Lula' Da Silva, declared that if every child in Brazil had an orange every day, there wouldn't be any left for export. This vividly illustrates the expanding market for food which the escape from poverty could bring. We have become obsessed, perhaps unnecessarily, with the competition to divide up what is seen as very much a finite market.

As Lord Selborne suggested in his Bledisloe Lecture (December 1992), 'We tend to accept that the market for food is relatively inelastic, indeed with the loss of export restrictions, we assume the market is declining, and we discount too readily the opportunities for new markets, whether for food crops, non-food crops, environmental benefits or other products for which the public might be persuaded to pay.' In that perspective, the battle to hold the line on overall production, or face the fallout from a totally free and unsupported market, may prove false alternatives.

It is clear, however, that it is incumbent on the richer countries to lead the way, and now is the moment to emerge from the hole into which we have dug ourselves. A determination to face such changes within the European Union could put a fresh emphasis on the questions raised by those countries wishing to join, and the more distant vision of a completely united Europe.

Within the European Union itself, a great deal of special aid has been given to less advantaged regions. In doing this, national jealousies and similar considerations have by and large been transcended. Meanwhile, the imposition of quotas to hold back production has had to be done across the board, without regard to the position of individual countries. In milk, for example, the UK has had to settle for a low level of production in terms of its own self-sufficiency, despite the fact that the industry is capable of further expansion. This may make sense in the short term, particularly when the question of subsidised exports still needs to be tackled. But when Neto, the Brazilian farmers' leader, criticised the present settlement in GATT, he also pointed out that support for Europe's farmers could be achieved without resort to export subsidies.

Some would take issue with this thesis, but it is the intervention system which can be said to have created the surplus. The present shift towards direct payments must involve an end to that system. Then lower market prices are accepted as a regulating factor, and intervention can only figure as some sort of insurance against disaster.

But what is it that opens hearts and changes attitudes if not a fresh orientation of the spirit? The Farmers' Dialogue at the Moral Re-Armament International Conference Centre in Caux, Switzerland put down a marker on this in January 1994. Although most of those participating were active in a great variety of farming organisations, they came as individuals to seek a purpose related to the world context. It became clear that the majority at least sensed that a sustainable agriculture is not so much a system as a farming community, with the standards and commitment which rest on a moral and spiritual foundation. That is the dimension which has been increasingly squeezed out of the picture, robbing us of our vision.

It was noticeable that a great number of those who assembled at Caux had taken part in exchanges between countries, and often in pursuit of a continuing relationship. They understood in some measure the people behind the statistics, and their way of life. That has always been at the heart of the European Union experience, though often political in-fighting has obscured it. At a time when the post-war reconciliation between France and Germany is increasingly distant history, it is interesting to see the publication, in 1993 of *Religion – the Missing Element in Statecraft* by researchers of the Centre for Strategic and International Studies in Washington. One of its case studies concerns the part played by Moral Re-Armament in Franco/German reconciliation in the immediate post war years, both in meetings at Caux and subsequent action in both countries. It documents the manner in which Caux became a key forum for an historical process which can now be judged in perspective. It suggests that the moral and spiritual development of our society remains the missing dimension of statecraft, and that without reconciliation, the pioneering political proposals would have foundered.

To explore that dimension has remained part of Caux's historic purpose, and its Farmers' Dialogues may yet prove a landmark in present agricultural policy. From a policy conceived purely in economic terms, the moral and spiritual significance of the farming way of life may be recognised afresh as a practical element.

Jan Oostergetelo, then a Social Democrat member of the German Parliament, declared his passionate conviction that in the European Union the spirit was the important thing, and regulations were very much secondary. Sceptical Swiss farmers gave unreserved support for their participation, if such a declaration could be proved valid. But, having established trust, the future will always remain a venture of faith. Yet faith in a new spirit which can be lived in daily steps may yet prove more tangible than faith in an economic process which can fluctuate wildly in the course of time, and much of which may lie beyond our immediate control.

The personal farming experiences and dilemmas shared on these occasions at Caux by farmers from different countries and situations, reflect the decisions that have to be taken immediately. But after every grasping of the nettle, there comes a moment when one asks oneself if one has made the right decision. As Lord Plumb wrote after reading the report of the 1995 Dialogue, 'I enjoyed reading the comments of some deep-thinking people, and the more I travel to poorer countries and witness despair and devastation, the more I think human dialogue is necessary. It is as Henry Heald sums up, recognising human relations and learning from our mistakes.'

Farmers are well placed to realise that, while eternal values must by definition be old values, they are infinitely renewable. So the title 'Real Choices' given to the NFU discussion document has a genuine significance. It is, above all, a choice of the immediate direction to take, not something that is for ever and irrevocable. Yet it is a choice which needs to be weighed up on the basis of principle and purpose. Whatever the shortcomings of our democracy, we are not powerless to fight our corner, though, of course, we may not immediately prevail. But the NFU is not the only organisation which has had fundamentally to adjust its structure, and go through the arduous labour of winning back the sagging support of its members. It is to be commended for sticking to its task with considerable tenacity, but there may now be a strong case for those who consider that the tenure of the President should be a fixed term and not depend on annual re-election. Having once been chosen, he must have the chance to develop the ideas for which he has won a mandate. That is a necessary basis for establishing consistent and effective leadership.

Under the pressure of today's circumstances, choices must be made which not only select the right direction in which to go, but also make the passage there as smooth as possible. In the European context, it has always been assumed that the UK, with its larger farm structure, would be disadvantaged by any measures of support related to farm size. But maybe it is time to think not so much of supporting the small farmer, but rather at what level the larger farmer should no longer need support. Any cut-off point, whether at 500 acres or even 1000 acres, is of necessity arbitrary. It would also be desirable to relate any upper limit to the number of people employed, since arable operations tend to shed labour, while livestock are more labour-intensive. Lord Plumb observed, in a speech headed 'Food for Reform' in 1990, that 'Rhetoric to the contrary, our policies have supported the commercial farm at the expense of the smaller family farm, while not stemming the flow of people out of farming'. This, of course, is because the commercial farm has been financed on the continued reduction in labour. It has been assumed that this represented increased efficiency, but that is an assumption which at this stage may be open to challenge. Certainly, the workers have not benefited commensurately with that rise in efficiency, which might have been expected to put wages on a par with industry. Nobody wants to put the clock back, but it would be premature to consider that there is no place for the smaller farmer in the future. For so long as there is substantial unemployment, he may be more efficient in economic terms than is popularly supposed.

But with the economies of scale which have led to expansion in the first place, there should come a point at which increased efficiency is able to face the full challenge of the market place. Since it is mainly from such units that production for export would be drawn, it could provide a good opportunity to measure the economics of the new situation which would be created. In that sense, it could be seen more as a recognition of efficiency than a discrimination against it. Up to now, nationalism has prevented the transfer of farm quotas across national boundaries, even with the advent of the single market. But those who are prepared to sell on the open market can increase their market share by perfectly fair means without the fetters of quota. They would still have support up to the basic level fixed, but could go beyond it because, under decoupling, such payments would be divorced from prices.

Now is the moment to make these decisions count, and to restore a measure of confidence in the future. The farmers' way of life has survived many onslaughts and continues to resist the complete takeover of materialism. The wide disparity in farmers' economic circumstances in different parts of the world is a challenge to our solidarity, as well as to our continued hopes of independence. With renewed confidence, the world's farmers may become a spearhead in the affairs of the new century.

Chapter 18
What Next?

Coming to the end of a century is always an excuse for looking ahead at the century to come. But even the frenetic character of today's world has so far failed to speed up history in any very meaningful sense. So, in speculating about the future, we remain aware that whatever we envisage may take many years to reach reality. It may truly be the shape of another century rather than a few decades.

The belief that we were automatically set on the road of progress has suffered too many jolts to have much grip on public consciousness today. Technical developments alone have manifestly failed to deliver peace or fulfilment, though they have clearly made life easier and more comfortable. All the talk about the development of communications super highways round the world is bound to raise the question of what it is we have to communicate. The irony is left hanging in the air that what we really understand is the wealth it will generate for those who lead the way.

In the British parliamentary debate on lowering the age of consent for homosexuals, which took place in February 1994, Edwina Currie was rash enough to invoke the 'civilised standards of Europe' as reason for us to change. Her speech, while lively as ever, provoked both echoes and dissonance in unlikely quarters. As always, the interest lay not so much in how people lined up on this particular issue but in the basis on which they made their judgements. I have never been a great admirer of Shakespeare's Hamlet, but I have always felt he hit the bull's-eye when he said to his friend Horatio, 'There are more things in heaven and earth, Horatio, than are dreamt of in your philosophy.' We spend a great deal of energy in passing judgement on the circumstances of the day, when we could consider the possibility of living in a different dimension. That is what a different philosophy could offer.

What harvest might a philosopher hope to reap in the years to come? It may remain an accepted truism that 'man does not live by bread alone,' yet the corollary, 'but by every word that proceeds out of the mouth of God' is now rarely even implicit in such a declaration today. We are ready to talk about spiritual questions, and even to accept the need for greater spirituality, but we are seemingly anxious to escape the authority of God. From there, it is but a small step to cutting ourselves off from that larger source of wisdom which could direct our steps into hope and fulfilment.

Fortunately, the idea of self-fulfilment as a worthwhile goal seems to be rapidly losing its appeal. It requires a massively self-centred arrogance to sustain such an idea to its logical conclusion, and there is in human nature a deep desire to be a part of something greater. But for those who do not find some God-given inspiration, it becomes increasingly hard to view the future in other than apocalyptic or gloomy terms, perhaps because imagination is baulked of the belief that dreams can indeed be translated into reality. Hence the formidable appeal of the National Lottery to all those who lack the entrepreneurial flair to become self-made millionaires. This is inherent also in what seems to be a popular revulsion from personal responsibility, and a horror that we should feel any personal guilt for things that go wrong. Repentance seems to be equated in secular thinking with stewing around in failures which cannot be redeemed. So I was interested to read in my translation of the Koran that 'Repentance means writing a contract with the future'. The Islamic view seems not only more hopeful but more businesslike.

Certainly, there remains a short and solid bridge between the golden vision and the somewhat earthy common sense so characteristic of the farming scene. The acceptable moral standards of straight living and straight dealing remain the basis of its construction. The wholehearted commitment of men and women remains its enabling factor. On such a foundation there should be an underlying certainty about the nature of the next chapter.

Ricardo Semler, in his book *Maverick*, details the revolutionary changes in his factories which have achieved so much, while flying in the face of accepted practice. His conclusion is, 'A company should trust its destiny to its employees... I hope our story will cause other companies to reconsider themselves and their employees. To forget socialism, capitalism, just-in-time deliveries, salary surveys and the rest of it, and to concentrate on building organisations that accomplish that most difficult of all challenges: to make people look forward to coming to work in the morning.' Yet even Semler does not fully unveil those hidden springs of motive which constitute the untapped resources of mankind. But it is those resources that we must employ if we are to match our technological advance with a real renaissance in the art of living.

Such a renaissance would inevitably alter the whole character of political and economic power, which has been shaped by the materialism of the twentieth century. It would end the age of superpowers and summits, preside over the rundown of the arms and tobacco industries, and accept environmental issues as part of the guide to good living. It would destroy the idols erected in the money markets and re-establish the goals of manufacturing in terms of meeting human need. Indeed, in the UK there is already a vibrant spirit at work in the revival of manufacturing industry. Current comments about the absence of the 'feel-good' factor can certainly be dismissed on behalf of those involved in the action. One phrase which particularly struck me at a recent industrial seminar was the proclaimed need 'to spread world best practice'. The implications have lingered in my mind since, with their supposition that the pursuit of excellence is something to be shared worldwide.

That phrase seems to contrast with a recent controversy over the selling of cut-price cigarettes in the supermarkets. Criticised by the BMA (British Medical Association) for selling them cheap, and under brand names other than their own, the spokesman of one big supermarket replied, 'We made a very definite decision not to advertise the product. But the launch of Benington provides customers with a wider choice of products at competitive prices.'

The spokeswoman for another said, 'Market research has shown that our customers do not expect to see our name on a tobacco product'. They seemed hurt at accusations of hypocrisy, presumably because they were following the accepted morality of the marketplace.

This might lead us perhaps also to meditate on the limits to competition in an interdependent world, or at the least to reconsider the aims of such competition. What comes next may be a more people-orientated development and a fresh recognition that the Western way is not the universal way. We shall have to meet head on the assumption that our technology, because it is at the frontiers of man's existing knowledge, is therefore the unchallengeable way ahead. We need to pause long enough to understand that if cultural traditions have survived hundreds or thousands of years it is because they reflect tried and tested values. The current confusion between love and lust alone ought to be enough to warn us that the role of sex in human society is very much less significant than the qualities of the spirit. The competition we should be seeking is very much more in the realm of ideas, where anything resembling a long-term purpose seems in danger of being crowded off the screen.

The rapid development of supermarkets and fast food outlets is but one symptom of this single-track thinking. The hapless pioneer soon finds he has created a massive bandwagon. Some go up-market, and some go down. Yet the final destination is barely considered. The spread of McDonalds around the globe is an extraordinary and established phenomenon. I have myself been numbered among its customers, but I hope and expect that it will be superseded by fresh values in popular eating. The multiplication of volume and the grinding down of margins may have become a universal technique, but other cultures will in time find other ways. Perhaps we should already be encouraging them to find expression, and to reflect on the value of friendship with neighbouring countries as a greater security than armed strength or even economic might. To consider seriously whether to be one's brother's keeper could deliver more than programmes on poverty. Perhaps most difficult of all would be to contemplate the end of hierarchies and the inauguration of a new dimension to democracy.

Do such thoughts prompt us to feel the need to come down to earth, or to make a serious attempt to explore the spiritual stratosphere? That should not be seen as a choice between reality and illusion, or practice and theory. It is rather a consideration of the discoveries which need to be made in the realm of the spirit, and which are unlikely to be made only within the four walls of office, factory, church or home, in so far as these are fixed points in our outlook. Our age has not been unmarked by faith, whether religious or secular. But faith alone, by its very intensity, can become divisive. Harnessed to love, it could become the generating power that is needed, not in some renascent liberalism, but in the harder currency of sacrifice, the fulfilment of those who learn to lay down their lives in service.

For such, the Commonwealth has always been a meaningful successor to Empire. To others, it seems more of a mirage, an insubstantial embodiment of a goodwill that rests only on sentiment. Yet the years have shown that it has its uses, and its achievements can be counted not only in diplomacy but in the concrete terms of education, scientific research and business enterprise. Certainly, the Commonwealth's Agricultural Society continues to flourish, and it is essentially a fellowship of learning from each other. The present Secretary-General of the Commonwealth, Chief Emeka Anyaoku, declared in a recent interview (*For a Change*, April/May 1996), 'The Commonwealth is a growing force for good in terms of its contribution to international affairs in the area of conflict resolution'. Unlike most other international organisations, the Commonwealth seeks to reach consensus at its meetings rather than take a majority vote. Chief Anyaoku maintains that this encourages action rather than rhetoric. He asserts that the meeting in Auckland, New Zealand, in November 1995, represented a gigantic leap forward in terms of its effectiveness.

In the same vein, the United Nations is now increasingly involved in altruistic operations on the ground, whether it be peace-keeping or relieving famine or an almost impossible combination of both. Bosnia may have provided more horror stories than successes to date, but there has also been unsung heroism, and commitment to principle. It is regrettable that the farmers' arm of the UN, the Food and Agriculture Organisation (FAO), has had a chequered history since the heady days of Sir John Boyd Orr's early crusade against hunger. Like many another arm of bureaucracy before it, it has been seen as unwieldy and expensive. But more than anything, perhaps, it needs a rejuvenated purpose and raison d'être, a transition from paper to people.

It is indeed a prolific source of statistics, but it has become rooted in Rome instead of being run by the people in the field, who are inevitably more aware of what is happening on the ground. Such things will no doubt be rectified but, for the moment, the more productive field would seem to be the growing networks of farmer-to-farmer action which have been described. For here have been planted the seeds of the new democracy, which will be directed by disciplined but popular (ie people) action rather than by government. But there could easily be increasing interaction between public and private initiatives, because that is what is needed to make democracy more effective as an exercise in participation.

In such realms, one cannot wander too far beyond the realities of today. But it is legitimate to suppose that a useful role lies ahead for the United Nations, both as peace-keeper and arbitrator. Undoubtedly, this will require much better preparation in terms of the scope of the operations involved and the training needed. Responses to disaster, whether natural or man-made, have often been heroic. Yet there still seems to be a certain reluctance to create the kind of body which could give a professional and multi-skilled response. The military, perhaps naturally, are inclined to feel that it will conflict with their readiness to fight a war. It could be, rather, that it needs to be part of the concept for a new role which matches changing times with changing tasks. It could be the beginning of a working vision to meet disaster and destruction on a genuinely international basis.

Politically, that vision has faltered in Europe, but it is at least to the credit of the European Union that the process initiated has created its own momentum which is not easily halted by setbacks. Smaller countries are taking the plunge of joining, and it is reasonable to suppose that they will be an added insurance against creating anything too monolithic. Diversity is only a complication when it comes to organisation. So it may be taken as an argument against too much organisation, while we examine the difference between an organism and an organisation: a body which is animated by life, and one kept in being by a set of rules, necessary though those may be. The Franco-German reconciliation remains a fundamental part of the foundations, but there is need for fresh expression of the cement required for a rising building. It is to this that I hope the farmers can contribute the establishment of a shared purpose.

The accession of Central and Eastern European countries will be the final guarantee of a united Europe, which will be proof against Balkanisation and the ethnic divisions of Nordic, Anglo-Saxon, Latin or Slav. Then the nation states will finally have abandoned dreams of empire and begun to look for a civilisation which could endure. In terms of a new economy, it may seem more than a little fanciful to look to the trans-national companies to change almost beyond recognition. Yet they do no more than reflect the values of the age that shaped them and now, from China to the most sacred halls of Western banking, it is beginning to seem that the one thing we can be sure of is that capitalism will have to learn to live in a climate of perpetual change. Settling down to a particular way of working may be a thing of the past, and known paths may be erased from the map. Certainly, one doesn't have to point the finger only at Shell to suggest that business leaders are rarely able to cope adequately with the introduction of a political dimension.

In such circumstances, the weakness of relying on a few highly-paid top executives may become more apparent. There may be a wisdom in breaking down big businesses into smaller units which does not rest simply on the thesis that small is beautiful, or even the desire to escape takeover! It may have merit because it allows greater flexibility and the taking of decisions closer to the scene of the action. It may even accord better with people who work at home, using their own personal computers, and it may also reflect the present tendency for most jobs to be created by small companies. When Ricardo Semler abandoned the pyramid structure common to most industrial companies, in favour of concentric circles, he formulated a change whose time had come. It simplified human relations on the job and made greater flexibility possible: things which people already hungered for. It threw into relief all the negatives which have accumulated with increasing growth, and which Semler labelled the diseconomics of size.

A valuable example, in this respect, has been set by Sierra Rutile (SRL) in Sierra Leone. A subsidiary of the US-based Nord Resources Corporation, which started activities in 1983, SRL is a dredge-mining operation for high-grade Titanium ore. A British engineer, Derric Hanvey, accepted appointment as manager on the condition that the company would give him a community development budget.

In the space of ten years, a specific Development Department has been created in the company, and a blueprint for the future produced, employing the expertise of the international agency CARE. This is known as the Environmental Masterplan, and it incorporates five inter-related programmes. Three of these are managed by the company:
- the relocation of villages;
- the rehabilitation of land;
- community development within the mining area.

Two are managed by CARE:
- the wells and village health programme;
- the Sustainable Agriculture Village Extension (SAVE) programme.

A close relationship has been built up both with local communities and national government. Chief Margai, whose chiefdom is a part of the mining district, says, 'I see Sierra Rutile as being very important for the future development of this region, and indeed the country as a whole... As a company, they have already made a substantial contribution, and while we inevitably have areas of disagreement, we have established an excellent dialogue, and know our point of view is always taken into consideration.' Two National Government nominees are directors of the board of the company.

The International Finance Corporation (*IFC and the Environment*, 1992) concludes with an assessment of the company's activities.

> SRL's management is keenly aware of the company's obligations and responsibilities in community development and environmental care. Lack of government services in the area has resulted in SRL's providing, at their own cost, such services as agricultural extension programmes, provision of health care and education facilities, training for health care workers, provision of clean water and other sanitation services to area communities, as well as loans to local entrepreneurs. SRL's current programmes go well beyond the requirements of current World Bank policies and guidelines for such mining projects.

It is sad, therefore, that in 1995 the Sierra Rutile mine was occupied and closed down by insurgents opposed to the country's military regime. With around 2000 employees, of which only 25 were expatriates, it was one of the largest employers in the country. Possibly the good work accomplished may yet ensure that this proves a temporary interruption.

Although no British farming companies are in the same league as the multinationals, I do find myself reflecting on the continued growth of farm size with some doubts about its value as the dominant pattern for the future. Time will tell, but there must be a size at which the continued balance of advantage will be called in question. Perhaps it is not simply an inevitable economic process, as so many accept, but rather the expression of economic assumptions which are about to be reversed. Yet if that is so, it awaits our decision and our perception of what it may mean to put quality of life before technology. There has been much talk of large companies providing a career structure, but the implication of that has been the chance to climb the ladder, rather than get established as a farmer. On the other hand, if the modern tendency is to have fewer managers and more foremen, does that represent greater opportunity or just a back-door attempt at economy by having a greater number at a lower salary level? Perhaps it is fairer to suppose that the future should not be entrusted to a single formula. That is what the 'market-driven' argument is partly about. Contract farming, which is a market-driven development, looks set to increase. But it remains to be seen whether the rising concern for full employment may not produce a change of direction. The idea should not take root that we no longer have the power to choose, however strong the apparent logic of current developments.

Suffice it to say that there are serious questions to be asked before one can simply accept that present trends must continue. The hundreds of millions of peasant farmers in Asia have yet to find their voice, and it is not for us to speak on their behalf. It is interesting to learn that The Household Contracted Responsibility System, now the official pattern in China, was pioneered by a handful of villagers when it was still against the law. Their faith in single families, even when it might have landed them in prison, was noticed, and fortunately appreciated by the authorities. But the changes to which it has unlocked the door are still in their infancy. They enshrine a respect for the individual which is immediately under pressure from the dash to get rich quickly but which is in turn counterbalanced by Confucian ethics, the traditional fabric of Chinese culture.

Bill Gates, the Microsoft computer chief, made some interesting observations in a *Guardian* article on a recent holiday in China (November 1995). 'As someone who usually spends his days thinking about how computers and communication will change the world, it was refreshing to be reminded that there is a large group of people for whom issues related to technology are not all that important. China is a country whose main resource is people. Eventually the skills of those people will be used more effectively because of computers. But for the next several decades most Chinese will be unaffected. A few hundred million will have their lives changed, but the vast majority will be consumed by other challenges. For them enlightenment about how to better manage farms will have a hundred times the impact of PCs in the near future'.

It has already been noted that the first reaction of those coming out of agricultural colleges in developing countries has often been that they now have the qualifications to command a good salary and the capability to direct others, rather than sweat with hoe or spade. Indeed, machinery has promised to make the latter redundant. That has been an orthodox Western attitude for so long that they are surprised to find many in the West still shedding some sweat, and certainly getting their hands dirty. They have not yet, in historical terms, had much opportunity to assess what a farming life can mean with the knowledge that opens new horizons and the pressure for survival lowered. It is to be hoped that that opportunity will be nurtured rather than cast aside, and that one struggle for survival will not simply be superseded by another.

Society has to come to terms with some new balance of forces which can accommodate productive farming without the overweening ambition to dominate. Small-scale farming in the tropics has already shown its potential for intensive cropping to be combined with good soil conservation. Education will develop this further, and it may not be too much to hope that the drift to the cities can be reduced to what may be a genuine reflection of excess population seeking fresh employment. Then, all those who have a chance to farm will see it as a fulfilling role, and one which remains at the forefront of human development.

Even in New Zealand, where people are proud to have achieved a farming industry virtually unsupported by subsidies, there have been tough battles for survival and diversity. But, as Gordon McConnell, Principal of Harper Adams College, pointed out at the Oxford Farming Conference (1996), New Zealand's well-worn path to farm ownership – share milking – is worth much more attention in Britain. Hard work should have a part to play in opening the door as well as ready cash. But each case must be treated on its merits, with answers which are appropriate to the circumstances. Australia is a case in point, where a difficult climate and deterioration in the terms of trade have badly stressed both farmers and their environment. The Australian Landcare Movement, and the many community groups which it has generated have begun to face up to these questions. They have raised morale and strengthened the belief that farming could and should provide a worthwhile way of life. But they have also shown that this depends on international farming solidarity, and the desire to get things right for the good of mankind, rather than simply point to pockets of success around the globe.

Moreover, even the bedrock faith of the United States in free competition is being tempered by the harsh winds that are blowing and the failure of large cities to maintain a human face. Many are still driven by a blind belief in competition and the security of being among the financial winners. But it will not be enough when it comes to saving the planet and, despite the official stance of the American Farm Bureau, doubts are creeping in on the farms themselves about the needs and welfare of the farming community.

Fortunately, at a moment of decline in world grain reserves, farms can again feel that they are really needed. In Western Europe we may feel a little apprehensive about the potential competition from former communist countries once they get their act together, but the real challenges ahead concern not so much territories as peoples. The joint pressures of population increase and advancing technology must be placed against the needs of the natural world. Man is no longer a spectator but a major influence impinging on the environment of our planet. So we must learn to view the future from this angle.

Farmers are in fact showing themselves more adept than might be expected in the business of crossing frontiers. This may lie partly in the artificiality with which many frontiers have been drawn, but probably even more with the universal nature of friendship as a global experience, where so much is held in common. In South East Asia, on the frontiers of China, Burma, Thailand, Cambodia and Laos, the movement of tribes and peoples has traditionally been fluid. Overlaid by politics and war as it has been, such freedom to mix might again become reality.

For farmers, the village remains the community. It can absorb newcomers exiled from their own homes or it can send out its own to earn a living in the city. Marketing remains a social occasion where people can mix freely and exchange intelligence through a good gossip. The growing bonds of international commerce may modify this situation, but probably not destroy it. For farming is one of those activities which can transcend national boundaries without weakening primary loyalties.

Political events, of course, have their impact. Today, Croatian farmers on the frontier between Slovenia and Croatia can no longer cross over for the part-time jobs on which so many depend in an area of small farms and high population. But that is a passing phenomenon, which will have no permanent place in the history of the region. More significant perhaps is the future of our cities and the vision of those who see urban man as the man of the future. Can a city of ten or twenty million and more ever achieve real cohesion? Many are at work today healing the scars of the inner cities and creating new concepts of community, but the weight of this experience may yet end in the ideal of a smaller city.

In the longer term, science can be expected to play a greater role, perhaps as an equal influence with politics and economics. It should be the source of those overarching concepts which can put current technologies in perspective. The old argument about whether arts or science provide the better training for the mind is surely outdated. But it is not enough for scientists to shelter behind their expertise when hard decisions have to be taken. Science has faced a major crisis of conscience in the development of atomic physics, and its potential for destruction. Now it has the chance to explore a more positive role. It is a role which empowers man but which should at the same time leave him conscious of a greater architect. Can we conceivably exchange the thought of what we might be able to do for the thought of what God would have us do? Certainly it would be folly to see agricultural research mark time or even diminish at a moment when considerable expansion is actually needed.

For my part, I see God as the essential link between knowledge and the understanding of its potential impact on mankind. The chief weakness of computer forecasts is that they are based on the projection of existing trends. Some of these may hold good better than others but, when it comes to human nature, the real expert is God. If the story of the apple in the garden of Eden has survived down the centuries, it is surely because it is an extraordinarily apt metaphor for what has happened. We have grown in knowledge and sophistication in a way which is constantly allowing us to conquer new fields, yet our moral progress has been at best spasmodic. The temptation to take the place of God has been overwhelming.

Biology – the science of life – and all the sciences associated with agriculture lead inevitably to the heart of the matter. It is indeed surprising to recall that my agricultural degree, taken at Cambridge in 1942, qualified me as a Bachelor of Arts rather than Science. But today, with biotechnology beckoning and talk of genetic engineering mixing expectation with trepidation, the picture is very different. To a farmer who is not a scientist, it is an endless source of wonder that the chemical composition of a gene should be exactly the same for plants, animals and humans. It suggests behind the immense diversity of our world an underlying unity: a concept at which we are only capable of guessing. Yet nearly all would accept that it is a concept worth pursuing, and destined to have a greater influence on the future of mankind than most of today's pre-occupations.

We may soon be coming to a genuine understanding of global

warming, and we are certainly in a position to rectify man's grosser sins of pollution against the environment. But we are still a long way from understanding, still less controlling, the ramifications of the carbon cycle, and the whole interaction of complex systems which assure the continuance of our planet. To face such need of greater understanding calls first for humility, and the realisation that as people we are under-performing amidst all the possibilities that life offers. Maintaining a high level of activity often militates against letting such a thought sink in. It is easier to form a new political party or develop a new economic theory than to understand what it means to make human nature our priority.

Ethical systems will certainly help, but it would seem that faith and love will also be an essential part of our armoury for the task. Perhaps above all is the need for the listening ear, alert to the promptings of a higher wisdom, whether seen as God, spirit or conscience, and seemingly implanted in every human being. That is the voice of the new democracy. It is the way in which everyone can actually play a significant part. Can we expect to take pleasure in a future without any guarantee of security, where the one certainty seems to be the promise of continual change? Only perhaps in the knowledge of a God whose spirit can lead us into all truth.

Note on Moral Re-Armament (MRA)

The 'World Mission', referred to in Chapter 3, came in the years of Moral Re-Armament's expansion worldwide following the Second World War. The great contribution to Franco-German reconciliation made when the Caux conferences began in 1946 have recently been documented by the Centre for Strategic and International Studies in Washington (*Religion, the Missing Dimension in Statecraft*, edited by Douglas Johnston and Cynthia Sampson).

> MRA's contribution was clearly limited, and just as clearly of proven significance. MRA did not invent the Schuman Plan, but it facilitated its realisation from the start. This is no small achievement, given the vast importance of every delay – and every acceleration – of the process of Franco-German reconciliation during those crucial formative years.

Dr Frank Buchman, the initiator of Moral Re-Armament, first used the phrase in a speech at East Ham Town Hall in May 1938. At a time when Britain was belatedly rearming to meet the threat of war, he sought to prepare people not only to stand against the wrongs of Hitler's regime, but to seek in that battle the moral and spiritual qualities capable of shaping a true peace.

He had already mobilised a substantial body of people committed to make real in their own lives the changes they wished to see in society. Absolute moral standards of honesty, purity, unselfishness and love focused the challenge of personal and global change. An early morning search for God's will in daily life was the basis for creative initiative and common action.

That has been the core of a work which embraces people of all races, creeds and backgrounds, but has no membership to measure numbers. Since the death of Peter Howard, a common leadership has been developed on the basis of consensus. National bodies, in which the work has been incorporated in each country, give MRA a legal form and status which can handle conferences, books, films, videos and finance. But the underlying commitment has remained the same: to be true to Buchman's original vision that MRA should be more an organism than an organisation. In that sense, it has continued to develop and grow without any concession to man-made definitions.

In today's world, MRA is working increasingly with the growing number of bodies concerned with reconciliation in situations of conflict, with the rebuilding of communities in the inner cities, the articulation and practice of a new industrial philosophy and the historical currents which are leading to a world view of the future for nations and individuals.

These will involve the wide field of inter-faith dialogue which has begun to seek understanding in terms of service, sacrifice and experience; but also, the now extensive networks of secular and humanitarian concern which campaign on a variety of issues, yet may need to free the hidden springs of motive to sustain a new spirit.

For those who have not had the opportunity to learn something of the background of MRA, useful sources of information are *Frank Buchman – A Life*, by Garth Lean and *Remaking the World – the Collected Speeches of Dr Frank N D Buchman.*

Enquiries can be addressed to MRA, 12 Palace Street, London, SW1E 5JF.

For a Change

This is an international bimonthly magazine read by subscribers in over eighty countries. Its editorial policy is to report on issues relating to community building and healing the wounds of history. It is published by MRA Productions Fund, a registered charity, at 12 Palace Street, London SW1E 5JF.

Bibliography

The Buddhist Way of Life, Christmas Humphreys, Unwin Paperbacks

The Land – Now and Tomorrow, Sir George Stapledon, Faber & Faber

Silent Spring, Rachel Carson, Hamish Hamilton

Proceedings of the Lenin Academy of Agricultural Sciences, July/August 1948, Foreign Languages Publishing House, Moscow

The Rape of the Earth, G V Jacks and R O Whyte, Faber & Faber

The Amateur Poacher, Richard Jefferies, John Murray

Anna Karenin, Leo Tolstoy, Penguin

Tolstoy – a Biography, A N Wilson, Penguin

Small id Beautiful, Dr E F Schumacher, Sphere

Witness For Ever, Michael Cassidy, Hodder & Stoughton

The Spectre of Capitalism, William Keegan

Maverick, Ricardo Semler

The Food System – a Guide, Geoff Tansey and Tony Worsley, Earthscan

Mahatma Gandhi – a Biography, Louis Fischer

Experiments with Truth, Mahatma Gandhi, J T Desai-Navajivan Trust

Rural China and Chinese Farmers on Their Way to a Market Economy, Professor Gao Lu and Professor Zhang Guilin

The Analects of Confucius, translated by D C Lau, Penguin

Minutes of the First Meeting, leading to the formation of the Farmers' Third World Network

Real Choices, discussion paper of the National Farmers Union, England and Wales

Frank Buchman – a Life, G D Lean, Constable

Peter Howard – Life and Letters, Anne Wolrige Gordon, Hodder & Stoughton

Religion, the Missing Dimension in Statecraft, edited by Douglas Johnston and Cynthia Sampson, Oxford University Press

Collected Poems, John Masefield, Heinemann

Handley Cross, R S Surtees

The Russian Question at the End of the 20th Century, Alexander Solzhenitsyn, Harvill Press

Alternative Agriculture, Committee on the Role of Alternative Farming Methods of the National Research Council, USA, National Academy Press

Crossing the Threshold of Hope, Pope John Paul II, Jonathan Cape

Sharpen the Sickle – the History of the Farm Workers' Union, Reg Groves, Porcupine Press

Gentleman's Relish, Edward Evans, Sapey Press

Index